Bruised by Belief

Bruised by Belief

From the Wounds of High-Control Christianity
to a Faith that Restores

Anu Matara

For Vesku, Max, and Mila

Table of Contents

Introduction..1

Part One: Recognizing Control for What It Is

Chapter One
Everyone Has a Story...7

Chapter Two
Laying the Foundation: Understanding Control.................11

Chapter Three
Signs and Practices of Control.............................19

Chapter Four
Emotional Control and Spiritual Bypassing.....................27

Chapter Five
How Language Shapes Culture................................35

Chapter Six
The World of Right and Wrong.............................45

Chapter Seven
When Relationships Mirror the System........................53

**Part Two: Recognizing Control by What It Forbids
(And Freedom Allows)**

Chapter Eight
Building a Healthy Inner House..............................65

Chapter Nine
Don't Be You, Be Perfect...................................93

Chapter Ten
Restoring Agency and Self-Leadership.......................105

Part Three: Recognizing Control by Its Impact

Chapter Eleven
Religious Trauma 119

Chapter Twelve
The Impact of Religious Trauma................................141

Chapter Thirteen
Bruised by Belief...151

Part Four: Rebuilding

Chapter Fourteen
Inner and Relational Healing....................................155

Chapter Fifteen
When Healing Requires Walking Away.......................163

Chapter Sixteen
Psychologically Safe Faith Communities......................179

Chapter Seventeen
Moving From Control to Freedom..............................193

Come to me, all you who are weary and burdened, and I will give you rest. Take my yoke upon you and learn from me, for I am gentle and humble in heart, and you will find rest for your souls. For my yoke is easy and my burden is light.
– Jesus in Matthew 11:28-30

Introduction

*"I've been so relieved to learn that all the trauma I sensed in me,
in moments when my pastor told me nothing was wrong,
was true, happened to me, and has a name."*

"I know I'm not supposed to want or need anything in life because my service to God is the only thing that should make me happy," Maria said with tears in her eyes. She had been coming for counseling for about six months, and we had made some real progress already, but now her old belief systems were fighting back hard.

"Are you happy?" I asked her. Maria had cried through every single appointment up to that point, and now her tears surfaced as she realized she, in fact, needed more than just her life in ministry. She needed to think about and reassess her dreams again and take some time off because she was exhausted.

All these natural needs were now at war with her learned belief system that screamed, "You're not supposed to need anything because serving in ministry has to be enough for you."

"No," she whispered. It was a significant truth to admit and be honest about. A cry of both grief and relief followed, and I waited in silence, nodding in understanding.

Following the rules of what was *supposed to* make her happy had actually made her exhausted, leaving her unable to navigate her own life and choices for quite some time. She had been stuck in a hamster wheel that dictated how she should think and feel, denying her permission to acknowledge how she was really doing.

The longer I have worked as a counselor, the more I have encountered exhausted, bruised, and traumatized Christians. When I first started seeing some clients as a student counselor, a bit over seven years ago, I didn't know that religious trauma was a recognized term. I started hearing stories of pressure, and people kept asking me, repeatedly, if they were still doing okay as Christians, having just missed a service due to tiredness. No one used the words control or abuse. Somehow, it wasn't possible that these amazing churches could also be the cause of their anguish. It must be them, and I would need to know how to help.

After starting as a full-time counselor, these clients kept falling into my lap. I know God led me in supporting them because I didn't know enough about the topic at first, but I knew I'd need to take it all seriously. I knew it was not "nothing," and I knew they didn't start any of this. I believed everyone when they shared about their crushing anxiety and fear of disapproval.

My understanding grew with my clients. I started studying religious trauma, cults, abuse, and high-control religion. I learned how to ask better questions from the people I saw and believed their experiences. I also kept making sense of mine.

My understanding grew, and my heart expanded. This is real, and this is important.

Maybe you have picked up this book now because you've experienced trauma in church. Or maybe you also believe this issue is important to talk about, and you want to learn more about it. Some of you might be leaders who want to care for their people better, some are just curious, some want to know what my angle on this issue will be, and some are reading this to be able to prove me wrong on some things. Whatever your reasons for reading may be, I'm glad you're here.

I have written this book especially for those of you who have been bruised by the control around you. This is my support for all of you. In the coming chapters, I will outline a path from first recognizing control to naming the wounding that often follows, to healing and building healthy faith communities, like this:

- **Part One: Recognizing Control for What It Is**

This opening section examines how control functions in practice—what it looks like, how it operates, and the forms it often takes in spiritual or relational systems. Through identifying key patterns and behaviors, you are invited to gain greater clarity and honesty in recognizing control in your own environment.

- **Part Two: Recognizing Control by What It Forbids (and Freedom Allows)**

Here, we explore how control is often revealed through what it restricts, particularly around questions, identity, and emotional expression. In contrast, we will also consider how freedom creates space for curiosity, authenticity, and wholeness.

- **Part Three: Recognizing Control by Its Impact**

In this section, we explore how control can also be measured by its outcome. We will focus on naming the emotional, relational, and spiritual consequences of controlling systems, and validate the often-hidden wounds that result from long-term exposure to coercion or manipulation.

- **Part Four: Rebuilding**

The final section turns toward recovery. It explores what healing from control can look like, and offers reflections on how to begin rebuilding lives, relationships, and communities marked by safety.

Scripture is clear about the invitation for us all to belong to a group of faith. I just don't believe we should ever use this invitation to keep people bound in unhealthy ones.

I have come to believe that we can assess the health of any system using widely accepted measures and evidence. The research findings in this book, for instance, are not mine, but come from multiple scholars who have studied control for decades. The ones I have chosen to present in this book can be found, in different intensities, in a wide variety of religious groups.

The stories I've chosen to share don't represent any one church or organization yet resemble one another in many ways. People I've seen over the years have come from different countries and different denominations, churches, and organizations. In these stories, all names have been changed, and some specifics have been altered to protect confidentiality. Even so, every story has been shared with permission. The quotations throughout this book, unless otherwise mentioned, have come directly from the people I have worked with.

This issue matters to me because I have experienced what I am now writing about. It matters because I've also heard hundreds of stories of shunning, shaming, pressure, and unrelenting external and internal standards for character. I've stood witness both to the pain and the healing.

As a clinical counselor with both specialized training in religious trauma and my own Christian faith, I have written this book for you who have experienced control in your faith environments and for your friends and family who may or may not understand what has happened to you. I have been writing especially for those of you who are recognizing the wounding in yourself but are still holding on to your faith in God. I realize this angle may be difficult for some readers who don't share the same faith as I do.

Even though I write as someone who believes in God and

reveres the teachings of Jesus, I also have a high regard for religious freedom. I live by a worldview that faith needs to always be freely chosen. I also believe in the power of education and believe that the best way to prevent abuse is to study it.

The truth is that the repercussions of control touch people far and wide. I am certain that if you are a Christian who knows other Christians, there are people in your vicinity who have experienced what I am writing about. Maybe you don't know this yet because they haven't been able to articulate it to you, or perhaps you have never asked.

I don't address all Christian communities, or all Christians, or name any churches or organizations because that is irrelevant to the objective of our learning. My goal is to help you recognize aspects of control with greater clarity so you can decide for yourself whether your community has become controlling or not.

While we will mainly examine the issues present in some faith cultures, I want to emphasize that many of our faith communities are healthy and safe. I am not writing about those cultures or the people thriving within them.

I hope that reading this book will give you more language to describe the things you or someone you care about has experienced.

Part One
Recognizing Control for What It Is

Chapter One

Everyone Has a Story

Now the tax collectors and sinners were all gathering around to hear Jesus.
But the Pharisees and the teachers of the law muttered,
"This man welcomes sinners and eats with them."
– Luke 15:1-2

"Our community's will would always overpower
the will of an individual.
The still, small voice of the Holy Spirit became too difficult
for me to follow when it went against the culture around me."

Everyone has a story, and this story of who raised us, where, how, and when, along with where life has taken us since, makes us all unique. These stories often contain key moments that change the trajectory of our lives or shape our thinking and belief systems in ways that may not serve us. Here are some of mine.

When I was six years old, I sat with other kids in a big white tent at a Christian summer camp. I remember looking at the teacher, who seemed nothing but lifeless and dull to me, claiming that Jesus had given him the greatest joy he had ever experienced. With dark circles under his eyes, he taught us about the joy of the Lord. How silly, I thought in my little mind, but repented right away. *Never criticize the one God has appointed to teach you. Keep your heart*

I can't remember how we transitioned into a time for questions and answers—this was a long time ago—but the speaker's wife, just as serious and tense, walked up. One of the kids asked her if it was a sin to go to the movies. I remember thinking I had been to the movies with my parents and watched films at home. What a silly question, I thought, and repented immediately. *Never criticize your brothers and sisters. Keep your heart humble and ready to learn.*

The wife decided it would be a good idea to give a cryptic answer to a group of six-year-olds. She said, "Maybe you don't need to think about whether it's a sin. Instead, consider that Jesus is coming back soon and whether you'd want him to find you at the movies when he does."

Silence.

First, I thought I would probably need to pray all the time, just stay in position, to make sure Jesus would find me on my knees when he returns. What if he came back the following week and found me doing something less important? Would he be offended? Leave me behind?

Then I realized the lady hadn't actually answered the question. How silly, I thought, and repented immediately. *Never criticize the one God has appointed to teach you. Keep your heart humble and ready to learn.*

Some years later, at a youth event, I was standing next to my friend when the main speaker of the evening told him that he needed to choose God right then, or the door would close on him forever, and God would never pursue him again.

My friend had been raised in a Christian family but apparently had walked away from the Lord as the speaker declared. And if he didn't choose God again that very night, he would end up living independently from him and go to hell. We were both 14 at the time.

I was terrified. What if the speaker was right? What if God

was truly speaking through him, revealing that for my friend, it was now or never? I stood there, paralyzed by fear for my friend's life. Not one critical thought entered my mind. The risk of the speaker being right about this overwhelmingly outweighed my ability to think for myself.

My friend was different. I remember him standing in front of that speaker, asking if he really believed God would say something like this to him and whether he thought it was a message from a loving God to his son. My friend wasn't angry or attacking; he was assertive, clear, and direct.

He seemed to be boldly challenging a leader, and I didn't think it was cool at all—I thought it was horrendous.

The speaker didn't back down, and I can't recall how their exchange ended that evening. My friend can't remember this whole ordeal at all.

Now, looking back, it is pretty clear that I had learned to believe that you should never challenge a Christian authority figure. Even if you had differing thoughts, you were expected to keep them to yourself, shut them down, and repent for even having them in the first place.

I still remember that this teaching was somehow linked to the Holy Spirit as well. It was believed that if you criticized a teacher, you might unknowingly be criticizing or mocking the Holy Spirit, which would mean you wouldn't be forgiven for your sin and would end up in hell. This seemed to be the ultimate consequence for most things, so it was better to avoid doing or saying anything that could risk your salvation.

For my friend, however, none of this crossed his mind. I was pretty certain he was playing with fire, because opposing what Christian authorities said was *not* something you did.

I am happy to announce that God has pursued my friend all his life, and he has pursued God. Since he was 14, he has had many opportunities to renew his relationship with God, reassess what he believes and why, and live authentically in his faith in Jesus. His direct way of communicating with anyone and everyone has also stood the test of time.

I know this because I have been married to this friend of mine for two decades now.

What I didn't know then, I know now: shutting down all my questions, thoughts, and even criticism that naturally arise within me can also shut down my discernment. If I adopt the mindset of listening to everything anyone tells me—because the rules around and in me say that I should never challenge a Christian leader—I risk prioritizing their words over God's wisdom in my own heart.

I found myself in vulnerable situations, listening to anything anyone told me. I believed words that broke me and accepted attributes that hurt me. This is precisely the position that enables religious control, and religious control injures people.

I was bruised by my beliefs.

***

Controlling faith explains **how we are supposed to think, feel, and behave** *if* we are truly following Jesus. It teaches that we should only think certain thoughts, feel a certain group of emotions, and want to say yes to select things *if* we really love God. Anything outside of these parameters would reveal that we are not truly surrendered as Christians. Over time, this can create an atmosphere where authenticity is replaced by performance, and inner struggles are hidden out of fear of judgment. Instead of being a space for growth and honest relationship with God, it becomes a system of measuring whether you are fitting the mold.

Because of these conditional expectations and the fear they can instill, some of us have carried the weight of religious trauma for a long time. There is a better way.

Chapter Two

Laying the Foundation:

Understanding Control

*Be shepherds of God's flock that is under your care, watching over them—
not because you must, but because you are willing, as God wants you to be;
not pursuing dishonest gain, but eager to serve; not lording it over those
entrusted to you, but being examples to the flock.*
– 1 Peter 5:2-3

"I started believing that first I have to do everything right,
and only then God can move in my life."

The first fundamental truth we will need to keep in mind throughout this book is that our spiritual health is tightly connected to our emotional, psychological, and physiological wellbeing. All these parts work together to make us who we are as individuals, and the Spirit in us pierces through all that we are. The better the integration between all these parts—our thinking, feeling, behaving, and believing parts—the healthier we are.

As Peter Scazzero says in his book *Emotionally Healthy Spirituality*, "Emotional health and spiritual maturity are inseparable. It is not possible to be spiritually mature while remaining emotionally immature."[1] This is true, and there is more; it is not possible to be spiritually whole and healthy while remaining disconnected from our bodies, from our thoughts and emotions, and from the whole truth of who we are as individuals.

If you have grown up in church, you may have heard the thought that "You are a soul and have a body." This, according to

---

[1] Peter Scazzero, *Emotionally Healthy Spirituality* (Zondervan, 2017), loc 28, Apple Books.

a wealth of research, is not entirely accurate. You are not a soul who just happens to have a body—you are an embodied human being. You are both body and soul, inseparably. Believing we are one or the other (or that one is more important than the other) can become harmful, because it teaches us to distrust our bodies or dismiss our emotional or physical needs.

All this will be important later as we go along together.

The second truth is that culture, whether within our family, nation, workplace, or church, shapes us profoundly. It can wound or heal us, often doing both at once. In *The Myth of Normal*, Gabor Maté argues that many modern illnesses are rooted in cultural dysfunction. Trauma, he writes, can be a predictable outcome of abnormal, unnatural circumstances. Therefore, it no longer surprises me that high-control religious environments often leave people wounded. After all, trauma can't be understood in isolation, because trauma is usually the visible wound of a systemic problem.[2]

This is why we will spend a good portion of this book exploring faith cultures that we may have normalized and gotten used to, but which reveal deeply ingrained systemic control and abuse, which is often quiet, subtle and discreet. It is also quite often, I believe, unintentional.

When it comes to any Christian environment, there is a healthy middle ground where we focus on creating cultures that are both psychologically safe and theologically sound. Psychological safety refers to an emotional climate where it's safe for everyone to take risks, express ideas, raise concerns, challenge and question, speak up when necessary, and admit mistakes, all without fear of negative consequences.[3]

They are safe environments because we can bring our whole selves to these places and the people in them, even the parts

---

[2] Gabor Maté, *The Myth of Normal: Trauma, Illness, and Healing in a Toxic Culture* (Avery, 2022), loc 8, Kindle.
[3] Amy Gallo, "What is Psychological Safety?" *Harvard Business Review*, 2023, hbr.org

of us that we are only learning to know and like, without any fear, because, "There is no fear in love. But perfect love drives out fear, because fear has to do with punishment. The one who fears is not made perfected in love" (1 John 4:18). In environments like these, we are able to relax and take our time.

Healthier faith communities show a willingness to learn how to integrate both Christian faith and psychological safety into their culture, while controlling communities may practice their faith "perfectly," but often do so at the expense of safety. It is similar to practicing faith in the "correct" ways, but neglecting justice, mercy, and faithfulness (Matthew 23:23).

Controlling faith can practically look different from church to church and group to group, but it usually shares these similarities:

1. It feels more important to be right about questions of theology than to remain in relationship with others. It feels appropriate to uphold black-and-white rules to test others, trying to catch them out, expecting them to be wrong in their beliefs, all while being "above" them. Control makes it difficult to recognize the unconventional moves of the Spirit while making it easy to spot "wrong" behavior (Matthew 23:23-24).
2. It is a culture of loaded language, where many spiritually-correct-sounding concepts are discussed with the help of Scripture, but where people's hearts may remain far from God (Matthew 7:21-23).
3. It feels right, appropriate, and even holy to observe whether other people are doing the right thing according to the rules and to report any shortcomings to their leaders (Matthew 12:2).
4. It feels important to do everything the way things have always been done, to follow the traditions and rules of the

faith community, and to consider anything different as sinful or wrong (Matthew 15:7-9).

5. It creates a perspective that judges everything different from them and everyone who, in their eyes, sins. Those who judge others believe they are doing the right thing by adhering to the rules and calling others out (Matthew 7:1-5).

6. With all this in place, it creates a culture where people are taught to care more about how they present themselves to others and how they appear on the outside, rather than being open and honest about what is happening beneath the surface, deep in their hearts (Matthew 23:25-26).

Control is baked into these cultures—and works like yeast. Jesus warned us about the influence of the Pharisees, probably because he understood how easily any one of us can begin doing "all the right things" while our hearts stay far away from him. What once started as devotion can over time shift into obligation and perfection.

Throughout his ministry, Jesus often challenged the religious leaders of his day and exposed how distorted faith can become when it is disconnected from love and authenticity. His words and actions continually pulled people back to the heart of God, instead of systems or hierarchies.

At the very heart of Christianity is a freedom movement started by Christ himself: a call to loving God with all that we are, and loving others the way we love ourselves. This kind of love cannot be coerced; it must be freely chosen. And it can best grow in environments that are safe.

Where Can We Find High-Control Christianity?

"**Control:** The ability or power to decide or strongly influence
the particular way in which something will happen
or someone will behave.

To order, limit, or rule something,
or someone's actions or behavior"
Cambridge Dictionary

High-control religion (or Christianity) can be found in groups that, in different ways, control, coerce, or abuse individuals' rights and freedoms. In these groups, people often feel they are voluntarily giving up their rights in search of a surrendered heart toward Jesus. They may not recognize the control behind the language and practices of the group, only their willingness to follow God with all that they are and everything they have. Anyone can be vulnerable to this, given the right circumstances.[4]

Control exists on a sliding scale, so it's not always abusive; sometimes forms of control are necessary and protective. Parents are meant to set boundaries for their children, and we are built to grow in self-control. In healthy relationships, we agree on shared control around housework, budgeting, scheduling and so on.

Control becomes problematic when it's one-sided and rigid. In groups of faith, control is abusive in nature when it limits the autonomy, agency, voice, or freedom of the individual and serves the needs of the controller at the expense of the controlled. When we begin to evaluate the health of our faith communities, we should learn to ask, "Who does this practice protect, the people

---

[4] William Chong, "Escaping High-Control Religious Groups," *Christianity Today,* christianitytoday.com.

or the institution?" All faith communities should examine this if their goal is to keep people safe. Control in groups of faith usually extends to how people are expected to think, feel, and behave, as well as what information they are supposed to accept or reject.[5]

In recent years and decades, there has been a growing body of research on religious and spiritual abuse and trauma. Even though these terms are nuanced and there is some ongoing conversation about how they should be defined, religious abuse is typically linked to organized religious institutions, while spiritual abuse can occur outside of traditional religious settings and may not involve any formal group. Religious abuse often focuses on enforcing adherence to religious rules, practices, or institutional structures, whereas spiritual abuse is more about manipulating an individual's personal spiritual beliefs and practices.[6]

All of this can happen in our mainstream churches. The increasing number of people who are being bruised in our faith communities has led to a surge in religious trauma research. More and more studies around the world are showing that **controlling faith environments are a major source of trauma originating in the Church.**[7]

And, unfortunately, controlling faith environments can be found all over the world, across all denominations, organizations, and Christian movements, even in ones that are popular, charismatic, and respected.

One of our first challenges in exposing control is this: it can hide very well, and in what we have normalized. It can hide in the familiar that we haven't learned to question and in communities that many have found great healing—these faith

---

[5] "BITE Model of Authoritarian Control." *Freedom of Mind Resource Center,* freedomofmind.com.

[6] Ellis, Heidi M. "Holy Hell, Religious/Spiritual Abuse and Attachment to God." Doctoral dissertation, University of North Texas, 2024. digital.library.unt.edu.

[7] Slade, Darren M., Adrianna Smell, Elizabeth Wilson, and Rebekah Drumsta. "Percentage of U.S. Adults Suffering From Religious Trauma: A Sociological Study." Socio-Historical Examination of Religion and Ministry 5, no. 1 (2023): 1–28.

communities are not all bad.

As I am not presenting any one church or organization in this book, I won't be able to talk about your exact situation. However, I pray you are able to take what helps you or someone you care about and work toward healing.

Chapter Three

Signs and Practices of Control

See to it, then, that the light within you is not darkness.
— Luke 11:35

"We're in denial of the culture we've created."

The word "culture" refers to the customary beliefs, social forms, and material traits of a group, while socialization is the process by which individuals acquire the knowledge, skills, values, and behaviors necessary to participate in society. As the authors of *The Church Called Tov* write, we can't underestimate the power of the culture around us:

"Choosing a church is choosing a culture,
and the culture we choose
will form us into the people we become."[8]

Throughout this book, we will examine some cultural red flags that I invite you to consider with honesty and accuracy. If you have shut down your questions before, I encourage you to stop ignoring the inconsistencies you may have explored and the discomfort you may feel about what you have observed. This won't always be easy, but it is important.

There is growing agreement across both clinical and academic fields about *the kinds of experiences that are most likely to cause religious harm.* The examples that follow are consistently found across psychology, sociology, theology and trauma studies.

---

[8] Scot McKnight and Laura Barringer, *The Church Called TOV* (Tyndale Elevate, 2020), Loc 116, Apple Books.

Researchers, clinicians and survivors alike have identified a recurring set of dynamics and patterns that appear across diverse religious and cultural contexts, indicating shared mechanisms of harm.

We will explore some of these in greater detail throughout different sections of the book.

People in these communities will probably feel **an unspoken expectation to uncritically accept their group's teachings as absolute truth,** with alternative beliefs seen as dangerous or misguided. Over time, this can lead to black-and-white thinking and such certainty where nuance and life's real complexities are denied in the name of faith. It often feels safer for people to stay silent when doubts arise within them, because challenging leadership or the group's doctrine is usually labeled as rebellious or spiritually immature, which can make it hard to speak up. Rational analysis, constructive criticism, or honest questions can often be dismissed, and other belief systems, or even different ways of practicing Christian faith, may be portrayed as unholy, sinful, or less than. All this can be accomplished by the use of loaded language and using Scripture out of context.[9]

In most cases, members are expected **to follow their leaders' guidance without any question or doubt.** The leaders of these systems are always seen as specially chosen by God, spiritually stronger, or more mature than others in their faith. In many high-control environments, obedience to leadership is seen as deeply tied to obedience to God, almost like they are one and the same. This can create a sense of fear or guilt around challenging authority or even thinking about leaving the group. Loyalty to the system and pressure to submit without hesitation can quietly take root in people, which can make it difficult for

---

[9] Hassan, Steven Allan. "The BITE Model of Authoritarian Control: Undue Influence, Thought Reform, Brainwashing, Mind Control, Trafficking and the Law" PhD dissertation, Fielding Graduate University, 2020. ProQuest.

them to trust themselves and their own discernment. These are cultures where trust in leaders is demanded, not earned.[10]

People inside and outside the system are divided into groups of **"us" and "them,"** depending on how well they follow the group's doctrine. Anyone who raises questions or challenges the ideas of the community or its leadership is wrongly labeled in different ways. They may be labeled divisive, offended, being under the spirit of accusation, mocker and scoffer, rebellious, or given any shaming term that makes whatever they say sound like an attack on God himself.

In these kinds of groups, teaching materials tend to come almost exclusively from within the community, with **little openness to outside perspectives**. Exploring well-researched topics, like psychology or broader theological viewpoints, can be met with suspicion or outright rejection. Members are often encouraged to stick only with what their leaders have approved, and they may be warned against listening to outside teachers, educating themselves through evidence-based subjects, or ever listening to current critics or former members of the group.[11]

These cultures usually place **high demands** on people. There may be strict expectations about how they live, how they practice their faith, who they spend their time with and how devoted they must appear to be. These expectations often touch every part of their lives: their time, energy, and personal choices. Many report feeling pressure to constantly be better.[12]

In controlling environments, the narrative tends **to place blame on members rather than on the leadership or culture of the group.** If people have questions, it might be framed as a

---

[10] Ellis, Heidi M. "Holy Hell: Religious/Spiritual Abuse and attachment to God" PhD dissertation, University of North Texas, 2023.

[11] Steve Hassan, Freedom of Mind: Helping Loved Ones Leave Controlling People, Cults, and Beliefs (Freedom of Mind Press, 2022), loc 27, Apple Books.

[12] Maria Björkmark, "From Broken to Whole Human Being: Suffering, Health and Caring After Religious Disaffiliation," Åbo Akademi University, 2023.

lack of teachability. If they feel exhausted, maybe it's because they haven't prayed enough. If they feel spiritually dry, the assumption is that their heart must not be soft toward God. If someone says no to serving, they might be seen as disobedient. According to this faulty narrative, the root of their struggles can *never* be in the practices, beliefs, leaders, or structure of their faith community—the problem is *always* them.[13]

In these environments, members often **begin to outwardly think, speak, and act in very similar ways.** Differences in opinion, personality, or even spiritual calling can be viewed as threatening or wrong. Over time, this can create a kind of false unity where harmony means total agreement, and honest disagreements feel uncomfortable or even dangerous. Many find themselves holding back parts of who they are just to avoid rocking the boat or being seen as "off track."[14]

In high-control groups, people are often taught that **certain emotions, like anger, sadness, or fear, are signs of spiritual weakness.** Over time, this can cause many to silence parts of their emotional life, afraid to express what they are really feeling in case they are judged by others. This kind of emotional control can lead to feelings of guilt and shame, making people anxious about thinking for themselves or experiencing freedom in being who they truly are. At the heart of this belief is a mistrust of their own emotions, paired with a trust in those who dictate how they should feel.

Often in high-control cultures, **mental health struggles or other life challenges are over-spiritualized** and real emotional and psychological issues, like burnout, anxiety, or depression, can be downplayed or dismissed altogether. In some groups, members may be told that these experiences are signs of weak faith, poor character, or a lack of spiritual discipline. Instead

---

[13] Alison Downie, "Christian Shame and Religious Trauma," *Religions* 13 no. 10, (2022)
[14] Laura E. Anderson, *When Religion Hurts You: Healing from Religious Trauma and the Impact of High-Control Religion* (Brazos Press, 2023), 180.

of being encouraged to seek proper care and support, many may be left feeling like their struggles are spiritual failures. This perspective can make it harder to access help when needed, and it often deepens feelings of shame or inadequacy. What is often ignored is that the environment itself may be causing the real symptoms of trauma or exhaustion that people are experiencing.[15]

All these practices, and some more, always **protect those in power and silence the suffering.**

Faith communities like these are unsafe. They offer people a list of how Christians are expected to think, feel and behave, but fail to teach how to have good discernment of character. As trust is expected to be given to leaders by their status alone, members don't get to practice the skill of discernment, nor are they given any time to grow in genuinely trusting them. People are expected to trust their leaders immediately, only because they are the leaders, not because they have proven their health to those around them. Many would have to turn off their inner compass to follow this expectation that is always framed as the will of God as well.

In their book *Safe People*, Dr. Henry Cloud and Dr. John Townsend speak about the issue of not knowing how to discern character.

First, they write, we will need to know how to recognize the unsafe ones, who:

- think they have it all together instead of admitting their weaknesses
- are religious instead of spiritual
- are defensive instead of open to feedback
- are self-righteous instead of humble

---

15 Tim Fletcher, "Religious Trauma: Power, Control, and the Lasting Impact of Spiritual Abuse," timfletcher.ca.

- only apologize instead of changing their behavior
- avoid working on their problems instead of dealing with them
- demand trust instead of earning it
- believe they are perfect instead of admitting their faults
- blame others instead of taking responsibility
- lie instead of telling the truth
- are stagnant instead of growing.[16]

Healthy people won't display all of these patterns, but most of us will relate to a few. Safe people can occasionally get defensive or place blame unfairly. They're also able to self-reflect and course-correct. On a sliding scale, the more often these behaviors happen and the more intense they become, the less safe the relationship can feel. People with a strong set of these characteristics tend to tell others what to do instead of listening. They can also start controlling others and build cultures based on outward appearance.

In her book *When Religion Hurts You*, Dr. Laura Anderson states that:

> "Abuse is, at its core, the improper use or
> treatment of something or someone...
> Abuse doesn't require intentional malice
> or harm. This is important because in
> many cases religious abuse is an
> extension of what someone has been
> taught is normal, acceptable treatment
> and behavior. For individuals who have

---

[16] Dr. Henry Cloud and Dr. John Townsend, *Safe People: How to Find Relationships That Are Good for You and Avoid Those That Aren't* (Zondervan, 2016), 28-38.

left HCRs (high-control religion), much of what we now consider abusive and harmful behaviors were first learned as spiritual practices, hierarchies, and disciplines, which were seen within the religious system as essential for living a godly life." – Laura Anderson[17]

Control, as listed in this chapter, is a form of abuse, the improper treatment of someone. Even in cases where this type of systemic control is unintentional and has gone unrecognized for years or decades, it remains harmful for the individuals in the system. By examining our realities as honestly and accurately as possible, we can become better informed and more equipped to understand what is happening in and around us.

We will discuss healthy (which don't need to be perfect) Christian cultures in more detail a bit later.

At this point, it is good to keep in mind that safe Christian church cultures actively work to prevent and address spiritual and religious abuse, control, lack of accountability and religious trauma. They want to learn about these issues and speak about them openly. Environments like these can become incredibly healing to people who have experienced the pain that follows after being controlled.

---

[17] Laura Anderson, *When Religion Hurts You*, Loc 38, 40, Kindle.

Chapter Four

Emotional Control

and Spiritual Bypassing

Do not let any unwholesome talk come out of your mouths, but only what is helpful for building others up according to their needs, that it may benefit those who listen. – Ephesians 4:29

"I have learned to shut myself down.
I don't listen to myself at all, I just do what is expected of me."

"I was always trying to suppress all of my emotions
hoping that one day God would take them all away."

In my life, I have often battled with sensing what people around me seem to be feeling and the mismatch with what they are saying. On multiple occasions, more than I could possibly count over the years, I have found myself perplexed about the gap between my lived experience and the language used.

For instance, I have been told that God's timing is perfect and when we truly trust him, we are not afraid anymore by those who I could tell were scared themselves. I saw it in their eyes and sensed it in myself while listening to them, yet there was no space to explore this further.

I would hear "before and after" stories when it came to faith. How, before following God, life would be filled with sadness and anger, but after following him, it has only been filled with joy and gratitude. This was sometimes preached from the stage even during painful real-life events such as sickness, stress and loss.

I saw it at that Christian summer camp, when the saddest man I had ever seen was teaching us about joy. Without understanding what was happening or having any other language than "silly," I knew back then, I picked up something authentic in him that didn't fit with the words he spoke.

What was left unsaid, in many of these occasions, was "I'm exhausted. I feel trapped. I need help. I'm not okay, and I'm scared to say this out loud." But I heard it. So often, I heard it.

For the longest time, this left me with only two options: either all these people are lying to me, or I can't possibly trust my own inner sense of what's going on in other people and the world around me. Maybe I can't sense what's real and what's not real at all. Or maybe I'm just not as spiritually mature as all of them. Every way I looked at it, I would end up with mistrust, either with others or myself.

I feel embarrassed to admit it, but at one point in time, I shared half-truths, too. People seemed not to question me further when I responded to them using faith-filled language. I did mean what I said, but at times, there was also a whole storm raging inside of me that I didn't tell them about. I hid it all behind my big smile but wondered if they were able to sense my sadness through it. Did they hear me like I had heard them?

Now I know this whole question is a lot more complex than just dishonesty. It's more about safety. It is about dysregulated nervous systems trying to stay afloat by hiding the parts of us that have been deemed unholy or sinful by the culture around us. It is about working hard to keep ourselves safe from unsolicited advice when all we need is support. The loud silence of hiding is more about fear of judgment in and around us than an attempt to be dishonest.

In healthy faith communities, emotions are welcomed as part of being human, but they are not demanded or measured as the "proof" of faith. In controlling communities, leaders create an atmosphere where certain emotions and their expressions are presented as required evidence of God's presence and believers' sincerity.

Emotional control like this is about regulating the entire range of emotional expression to fit the group's culture. It shows up in ways that are both overt (explicit rules and sermons about emotions) and covert (unspoken norms, social pressure and internalized shame). In these communities, emotions are categorized and divided into those that are celebrated and those that are silenced. This categorization begins with a fundamental distinction between what has been deemed acceptable and unacceptable to feel.

Sanctioned emotions are often joy, gratitude, excitement, peace, and sorrow for sin (especially one's own). These emotions are usually equated with great faith or closeness to God. In contrast, prohibited and suppressed emotions and internal experiences can include anger toward leadership or God, doubt, grief that questions God's goodness, exhaustion, or excitement about non-church pursuits. These emotions are usually framed as sinful and fleshly, rather than perfectly natural.

The suppression of these "unacceptable" feelings is frequently spiritualized and masked behind loaded language that discourages honest self-reflection. Emotional struggles of any kind are often reframed as spiritual failings, not as natural, human experiences. Instead of being given space to feel and process, members may often be encouraged to replace their emotions with a Bible verse or a "praise report" immediately, which may force them to skip their emotional processing entirely.

This can lead to a culture of emotional policing. If someone raises their voice, cries "too much," or is upset, it's usually treated as a character flaw. Public displays of vulnerability and honest emotion are often only acceptable during worship, or if they follow *the testimony script*: "I used to feel sad, but then God delivered me."

Guilt and shame can then become powerful, internal watchmen that enforce conformity. If someone feels hurt, it's often reframed as offense, unforgiveness, pride, or them being too sensitive. Expressing doubt or anger can be portrayed as "hurting your witness," "grieving the Holy Spirit," or leading others astray. This framing punishes transparency and makes emotional honesty look like sin.

In this kind of environment, emotional conformity becomes proof of holiness, and constant cheerfulness can be seen as a sign of spiritual maturity. Emotional distress, on the other hand, can be seen as evidence of hidden sin. If someone wants to feel like they belong in a group like this, they may need to learn how to perform positivity. They must learn how to show up as "on fire for God" and "walking in victory."

A culture like this can start to shape how people experience themselves and their own humanity. It creates a performance culture where the honest and true inner life must be constantly perfectly managed and hidden from others.

Very often, this results in a deep sense of loneliness and shame. The tragedy is that the God who weeps, laments, and expresses righteous anger is replaced by a shallow version who expects us to only stay silent and rejoice. Culture like this makes us forget that he is compassionate and has promised to tend to the wounds of our broken hearts (Psalm 34:18).

Over time, all of this can lead to suppressing unacceptable emotions due to fear of being judged. Chronic suppression can lead to physical illness, exhaustion, emotional numbness, delayed processing, and explosive private outbursts when suppressed emotions eventually surface. Without a connection with our emotions, we are unable to know who we truly are.

In his article on Redecision Therapy, licensed psychologist John McNeel discusses the internal "Don't Feel" message this way:

> People create a deeply flawed model of
> security demonstrated by almost
> superhuman qualities. They aspire to be
> someone who is more Teflon than
> human, thus not harmed by slights or
> adversity. They have a response for any
> situation and are master of their
> feelings... Lacking good models for what
> healthy security looks like, their eye is
> drawn toward other "superman" types
> whom they aspire to imitate (or conquer),
> never recognizing the core of insecurity
> that such behavior actually reveals. –
> John McNeel[18]

Alyson Stone, in her research *Thou Shalt Not*, discusses emotional suppression and its consequences in controlling faith communities this way:

> Prohibitions against entire categories of
> emotions can contribute to psychological
> difficulties, including depression, anxiety,
> guilt, and addictive or compulsive
> behaviors. In a similar fashion, the

---

[18] McNeel, John R. "Understanding the Power of Injunctive Messages and How They are Resolved in Redecision Therapy," *Transactional Analysis Journal* 40, no 2 (2010).

intellectual realm can become restricted,
promoting legalistic, black-and-white
thinking and difficulty with free
association, fantasy, creative thought, and
problem solving. – Alyson Stone[19]

Spiritual bypassing is a form of suppression that refers to a tendency to use spiritual explanations and practices to avoid addressing unresolved emotional problems, past wounds, unfinished developmental tasks, and complex psychological issues. Therefore, it acts almost as a shield, allowing individuals to hide behind spiritual explanations rather than engaging with their own or others' painful emotions or trauma. This approach simplifies the complexities of our psyche into oversimplified answers.[20]

Rather than confronting difficult emotions, people may focus on appearing "at peace" while avoiding the deeper emotional work that could lead to awareness and healing.

In practice, as Dr. Robert Augustus Masters in his book *Spiritual Bypassing* explains, this often shows up as "delivering one-liners with minimal feeling" and "employing spiritual beliefs to avoid dealing in any significant depth with our pain and developmental needs."[21]

It can sometimes be challenging to recognize when spiritual language or practices are used to avoid pain. For example, people may be told, or tell themselves, to "just pray more" in the face of emotional struggle. Prayer and Scripture are vital for those who want to grow in faith, but they can also become a shield to avoid confronting the harder realities of trauma and grief. When

---

[19] Stone, Alyson M. "Thou Shalt Not: Treating Religious Trauma and Spiritual Harm With Combined Therapy," *Eastern Group Psychotherapy Society 37* (2013): 323–37.
[20] Raab, Diana "What Is Spiritual Bypassing?" *Psychology Today,* 2024, psychologytoday.com
[21] Robert Agustus Masters, *Spiritual Bypassing: When Spirituality Disconnects Us from What Really Matters* (North Atlantic Books, 2010), 9-10.

spiritual practices are used in this way, the result is often disconnection from the most honest parts of the self. Avoiding pain may feel like the faithful thing to do, but it can prevent the invitation to heal over time.

The issue is not with prayer or Scripture themselves, but with how they are applied. These practices are meant to draw believers closer to God, not further away from their own hearts. A healthier approach holds both of these realities together: the need to pray and the need to feel, the desire to seek God and the courage to be fully human. Prayer is not an escape but a place where God can meet people in their hurt, exactly as they are, not as they think they should be.

People who have learned to spiritually bypass themselves and others usually:

- avoid feelings that bring them discomfort, such as anger, sadness, and fear, labeling them as sin
- struggle to tolerate other people's emotions that they have categorized as negative
- feel detached from parts of themselves and hold extremely high expectations of themselves
- believe that every difficulty, wounding, or traumatic event comes from God and is meant for their growth and learning
- focus solely on spiritual disciplines while neglecting their internal world, and fail to honestly evaluate what is happening in and around them
- believe in their own spiritual superiority as a way to hide from insecurities
- pretend that things are fine when they are not

- believe that people can overcome their problems through positive thinking
- repeat spiritual platitudes without thinking if it's just a way of dismissing difficult situations, so they can feel better[22]

When faith communities demand certain emotional expressions or dismiss difficult feelings, people learn to distrust their own inner experiences. This can start to create an environment where individuals feel pressure to present only what has been deemed acceptable, rather than what is true.

Healthy environments do not fear emotions, nor do they exalt them as the only sign of God's presence. These communities know that honest expression can lead to authentic healing. They also recognize that connecting with God can involve our intellect, where we thoughtfully engage with Scripture and grow in our understanding of the Bible. Faith is not measured by outward emotion but can grow in both the heart and mind, always rooted in truth.

---

[22] Cherry, Kendra "Spiritual Bypassing as a Defense Mechanism," *Very Well Mind,* 2023, verywellmind.com.

Chapter Five

How Language Shapes Culture

Do not lie to each other, since you have taken off
your old self with its practices
and have put on the new self, which is being renewed in knowledge
in the image of its Creator.
– Colossians 3:9-10

"Even when I was crying, asking for a break,
and telling my leaders I needed to go home,
I was told that I was changing the world and shouldn't give up now."

One cultural aspect of controlling faith environments is its specific language. Sometimes, our way of speaking can become *loaded.* Loaded language is a recognizable way to use words and phrases with strong connotations, both positive and negative, to invoke an emotional response in the listener. This type of language can influence the listener's perception of reality by triggering emotional reactions.[23]

Loading the language is like giving certain words a little extra "weight" so they hit harder or stick longer. Think of words like *freeloader, radical,* or *heroic* (random selection, I know!). They carry some emotional punch and can be powerful in storytelling or persuasion.

Loaded Christian language works the same way, but with words and phrases that are especially meaningful in faith communities. Terms like *anointed, blessed, excellence,* or *Spirit-led* can

---

[23] "Framing the world through loaded language," Calenda, *Interstudia Journal*, no.27, 2020, calenda.org.

carry spiritual weight, and depending on how they are used, they can inspire or alienate.

Loaded language becomes harmful when the whole group starts interpreting or using words in new ways that differ from the rest of the world. This kind of language can serve to alter members' thought processes to conform to the group's way of thinking. Such words and phrases compress complex problems and real issues into brief, definitive-sounding phrases, which are easily memorized and expressed. Language like this, therefore, is highly categorical, abstract and relentlessly judgmental.[24]

This is where loaded, Christian language can sound noble, divinely ordained and even loving, but is filled with absolutes and non-negotiables.

There are many words and phrases I could pick here for you to ponder on, but here's a start. Read through this list and think if they carry some extra meaning in your faith community:

- Faithful, called, obedient, surrendered
- Submissive, spiritually disciplined, pure, set apart, on fire for God
- All in, full of faith, sold out for Jesus, unshakable
- Slanderer, backslider, worldly, rebellious, mocker, scoffer

Who decided these categories? And how do you know where you stand?

In an environment like this, many learn to believe the narratives of their faith community over their own experiences. The narrative may say their doctrine is *straight from the throne of God,*

---

[24] Robert Lifton, Thought Reform and the Psychology of Totalism: A Study of 'brainwashing' in China (The University of North Carolina Press, 1989), loc 555, Kindle

their leaders are always *chosen by God*, and people who resist their rules are *enemies of the church*. If this language becomes their compass over what they can see, hear and witness, it can start to distort their understanding of reality. Using this language can become a way for controlling leaders to remain in power.

Language creates narratives, and in high-control groups, narratives need to be followed.

According to Amanda Montell, the author of *Cultish*, loaded language is commonly used to:

- Create community and solidarity
- Establish an us and them
- Align collective values
- Justify questionable behavior
- Instill ideology
- Inspire fear[25]

Instilled fear can create behavioral requirements that can remove individual choice and freedom. Any type of "have to" can sever the development of one's own will. Making independent choices can become impossibly hard in an environment like this.

High-control framing often presents choices as personal, but then attaches moral, spiritual, or eternal stakes to them so that any other option starts feeling like the wrong one to make. High-control choice framing can sound like this:

"If you truly love God, you will marry within our group."
"Godly parents protect their kids from secular influences, so you won't let them go to public school."
"If you trust God with your finances, you show it by not pursuing

---

[25] Amanda Montell, *Cultish* (Harper, 2021).

a career."

"If you trust God as a healer, you won't rely on worldly medicine."

"If you truly love Jesus, you will serve in ministry."

"Faithful believers attend every service and event; missing one shows your priorities aren't right."

"If you are humble at heart, you will never question our leadership's decisions."

All spiritualized threats sound like concerns for your soul, but are always control in disguise. This kind of language spiritualizes human control and makes people and their authority equal to God's will.

With this moral scorecard all high-control groups offer, independent choices move from freely made to doing things "right" or "wrong." For example, someone may genuinely prefer to attain a higher degree and a successful career instead of being in full-time ministry, but when the whole community frames all work outside of church as "worldly gain" or "selfish ambition," the genuine preference can suddenly start feeling less spiritual and wrong to the person.

This is where the inner battle begins. On one side are the individual's authentic desires, needs, and limitations, while on the other is a whole belief system that says rejecting the group's prescribed path to holiness means rejecting God himself. Even if this person moves forward with their life in ministry, the internal conflict continues in different ways. They may pour their heart and soul into service and an enormous amount of energy in doing it "right," yet never fully feel that things come easily or life flows freely through them. Because the choice that was framed as a test of Christian character, any difficulty they now face, or lack of enjoyment, feels like spiritual failure. In a culture like this, it usually doesn't occur to people that the choice itself was a poor fit to begin with and made under pressure.

Over time, a dynamic like this can breed chronic self-blame, suppression, and low self-worth. Instead of questioning if being in full-time ministry was ever their true calling, they assume the problem is their own lack of spiritual discipline. The original coercive framing vanishes into the background and is replaced with a persistent belief that says: *If I were a better Christian, this would be easier for me.*

It is difficult to abandon such a belief system, because the template given may very well represent someone's aspirations and goals as a devout follower of God. This is one of the ways high-control systems keep people locked in cycles of striving without satisfaction; the choice was never free, yet the burden of failure is carried entirely by the individual.

Burnout in Ministry

"For me to be accepted in church,
I have to please people."

I once did this simple exercise with Sarah, who had come for a few sessions because she was exhausted but couldn't understand why. She worked for her local church and shared how everyone around her seemed okay, except for her.

As I began to learn about her surroundings and the culture she was in, I realized that most communication in her faith community relied on loaded, Christian language. This became clear when I asked her to describe her normal work week for me; she used phrases like "I am learning how to surrender to God more," "I am partnering with what God is doing in the world," and "I have prioritized loving him and loving people over everything else."

As a firm believer in making things visible and concrete, I asked Sarah if she would like to write down her schedule on paper for me to see (and for her to see, though I didn't say that out loud). She began constructing her entire week in practical steps, from the moment she woke up to the moment she went to bed, seven days a week: prayer groups, mercy ministry, meetings, planning, and other responsibilities she attended to.

After adding it all together, it turned out she had been working around *70 hours per week for months without any breaks.*

She sat in silence for a long time as this realization was sinking in. This was another side of the truth she hadn't seen, buried under good intentions and a willing heart. Her perception of her own life had been obscured by the use of loaded language rather than the truth of what was happening in real time. It was a very different reality to acknowledge that she was part of an organization that, instead of "inviting her into a life of wholehearted surrender," was actually "not protecting her from burnout by making her overwork."

And yes, both of these statements can be at least partially true at the same time but not in equal measure. One was almost poetic, the other measurable. One sounded holy, while the other was devastating her body. She had always believed she was serving God with passion and with the kind of devotion that didn't count the cost. But now she could see that the language she'd trusted had been used to *sanctify exhaustion.* What she had learned to call "laying down her life" was, in reality, a system that had taught her to ignore her own limits and all the early signs of burnout.

Sarah had been praying for supernatural strength for weeks, as she had noticed getting (understandably) increasingly weak and weary. Her faith community had kept encouraging her to persevere. People had told her how "God always equips the ones he calls" and how "his peace would surpass all understanding" if Sarah just kept trusting him. The challenge was that these legitimate biblical principles were used to ignore her honest disclosures and not check the parameters of the work that had been laid out for her. Sarah's first logical conclusion in this environment was that she was doing something wrong because this was *not* how she was feeling.

During therapy, Sarah realized that she had known how bad she had felt for a long time, but because people around her wouldn't accept her emotions as they were, she had kept suppressing them and pushing them aside. Even though it was a painful realization, she concluded that she needed to take a break from ministry and start recovering from burnout. Some years later, she is still on that break.

What Sarah went through shows improper use of both language and Scripture. Yes, God does promise us these things, but it does not mean we are exempt from responsibility in protecting our health, boundaries, or the people who work for our organizations or churches.

The language of Christian concepts can be difficult to resist because most of us would quite naturally believe in them, but it is the practicalities of these concepts that matter way more. What do we mean when we say certain things, especially if we have started mindlessly repeating them?

In these environments, people often report feeling guilty and ashamed of themselves if they struggle to respond in the expected ways. Their own feelings and boundaries start mattering less and less, as they are usually painted as sinful and selfish, and saying yes to everything that is asked of them becomes the proof of surrender and obedience.

We should refrain from using loaded, Christian language and become honest and accurate in the way we communicate. Like in Sarah's case, we should also never diminish someone's personal suffering, or our own, into concepts of some kind, and respond to pain with spiritual bypassing.

As Lilian put it in one of our sessions: "It didn't matter at all what happened to me, as long as it was for God." This is what trauma can sound like.

Name the Control Narrative

"I was praised when I pushed through things
that absolutely broke me."

When harmful behaviors are masked under spiritual language, it becomes more difficult for people to name what's really happening. Naming things accurately is an important step in breaking free from confusion. The following examples show how damaging practices are often mislabeled, and what they are truly called.

If someone:

- forces other people to do things they are not ready for or don't want to do, the appropriate term to use is coercion, not encouragement

- polices other people's personal decisions and internal worlds, the appropriate term to use is control, not discipleship

- warns people that God will abandon or punish them if they step outside the system, the appropriate term to use is intimidation, not love or care

- twists someone's emotions, fears, or hopes to make them comply, the appropriate term to use is manipulation, not leadership

- tells people to cut off their former outside relationships and perspectives, the appropriate term to use is isolation, not purity or harmony of the group

- discourages or punishes someone for raising questions or doubts, the appropriate term to use is silencing, not obedience or submission

- minimizes or denies someone's lived experiences of harm, the appropriate term to use is gaslighting or victim-blaming, not biblical correction
- labels people as rebellious, unspiritual, or ungodly, the appropriate term to use is shaming, not accountability
- trains people to accept beliefs without question while denying diverse perspectives, critical thinking, or access to wide-ranging resources, the appropriate term to use is indoctrination, not teaching

Learning to call these practices by their proper names is important and exposes the disguises that keep the harm going. Naming things truthfully can stop us from accepting mistreatment and help us to move from the distortions of high-control systems towards genuine, freely chosen faith.

Loaded language can enter in, attempting to erase our whole lived experiences and make us question what we are very presently living through. It tries to sanctify suffering and reframes abuse as "holy."

This is the world of explaining the pain away, shared by many of my clients:

"Every time I was sad, or even tired, I was told I was 'refined by God' or 'the enemy's voice was in my ear.'"

"When my leaders asked me intrusive questions about my sex life, they called it accountability."

"I was told I was 'convicted' when I brought up issues about how we were led. It was turned around from me having real concerns to being convicted by God for my own sins."

"I couldn't get up one day because I was so exhausted. My leader walked in and said that God had told her I had been disobedient and now he was teaching me a lesson."

"Whenever I felt upset, I was told to fight off the spiritual attack."

Truthful words help restore clarity and dignity in people's lives. When we call things what they really are, we begin to see ourselves and others, even God, more clearly. We need to speak the truth even when it brings us discomfort and test the immovable parameters of our own belief systems that may not accept suffering, pain, mental health issues or other people's emotions as they are.

We also need to learn how to listen to people explain their own experiences and give them accurate language to explain what's happening in their lives. When I explain to my clients that what they are sharing with me sounds like control and trauma, it resonates in their hearts as the truth. It brings a certain level of relief alongside the pain and gives them permission to hold on to what they know happened to them, but the culture around them tried to rob from them. Speaking the truth brings freedom, where loaded language holds captive.

Chapter Six

The World of Right and Wrong

And this is my prayer: that your love may abound more and more in knowledge and depth of insight, so that you may be able to discern what is best and may be pure and blameless for the day of Christ, filled with the fruit of righteousness that comes through Jesus Christ - to the glory and praise of God.
– Philippians 1:9-11

"You can't think of your needs because
you're supposed to lay down your life for others."

When we listen to the language around us more intently, we may start to notice that sometimes we are only offered two opposing options. This is very common in high-control environments.

James walked into my office, visibly distressed. He had decided to be honest with me from his first session on and was now battling with the reality of this decision, sitting right across from me.

He started, "For all my life, I've been told that Christians don't need counselors. Even up to this point, before I secretly booked this session with you, I was told that Christians should seek help from either people who hear from God or from professionals." He paused for a moment, gathering his thoughts. "And of course, you should always go to people who hear from God, because others can't be trusted. I don't know if that's true anymore, but I heard you are a counselor and a Christian, so I booked."

I thanked James for his honesty. He had been brave to share his thoughts with me and to book his session despite all his previous learning. I didn't start challenging his beliefs or what he had been taught, as my job isn't to dictate what anyone should think. I knew he would arrive at his own conclusions if he gave counseling a fair chance. And he did.

The first step toward his ability to think independently was the realization that there was a real person sitting in front of him in a counseling office, who potentially embodied both of these aspects that weren't meant to belong to just one person.

After some time, James was able to recognize the controlling nature of his previous, dualistic thinking. Here is what we concluded after working together:

• Needing to choose between help that is either Spirit-led or professional is completely artificial and unnecessary. You can receive both, neither, or anything in between.
• Since this applies to both professionalism and faith, it can also be true for other extremes, which can likewise be evaluated with accuracy, examined with honesty, and measured with integrity.
• Thinking in terms of either/or often reveals control. Freedom, on the other hand, often sounds like both/and.

The truth is that, instead of only two opposing options, we have multiple healthy choices available, all of which lie somewhere on the same continuum. There exists a middle ground often absent in controlling systems, but it is readily accessible to us if we choose to seek it.

We are not limited to either total faith or complete doubt, perfect peace or overwhelming fear, or absolute strength or total collapse. The richness of real spiritual life can be found in the space that doesn't always have clean edges. I believe that it's in these sometimes unsteady, grace-filled middle grounds where we are offered the opportunity to grow the most. The tension in between is where true transformation can happen.

In such tension, we might find ourselves holding

questions and hope in the same breath. We might love God deeply and still feel confused about what he's doing and when. These don't need to be looked at as contradictions to be fixed, but as honest, human experiences to be named and brought to God with transparency.

The same mechanism can sometimes be seen in our belief systems. We often carry an unspoken assumption that our beliefs must be fully formed, unwavering, certain, and airtight. By believing this, we may start creating an internal world that doesn't tolerate any discomfort, so we push it away as far as possible.

When a belief system demands certainty, something inside of us begins to tighten. Certainty offers us an illusion of safety by making the world feel ordered, controllable, and explainable. What we don't often realize is that the cost of certainty can be internal fragmentation. Some parts of us will stay hidden and afraid when our internal expectation is that of perfection.

The truth is that life is not always neat or easy to explain. Suffering doesn't always make sense. Irene once shared with me how she had been told, by well-meaning but inflexible Christians, that she had been leaning on "the powers of darkness because she had allowed herself to have flashbacks."

Flashbacks are sudden, intense relivings of past traumatic events and are a common symptom of PTSD. Their belief system, however, didn't allow them to understand trauma or tolerate pain. It didn't allow space for healing that took time. It was either faith or suffering for them. Nothing in between, no middle ground.

Irene had lived through more pain than most of us could ever comprehend. Her story needs to be told, but not here, and not yet. Her story of unimaginable pain that lasted for 20 years until her escape from her traffickers left her with complex trauma. This is the natural side of life, and her nervous system still reacting in predictable, human ways to the horrors she went through. This does not cancel the love she has for Christ in any way. What she was met with was certainty paired with lack of knowledge. The truth is that trauma and faith can, and often do, coexist.

In healthy environments, all these things can be held together. We can learn to recognize that self-reflection and faith don't cancel each other out but support growth. We can learn to accept that our faith can be deepened, not threatened, by honesty and critical thinking. Healthy faith can hold both trust and questions, devotion and personal discernment, and self-awareness and surrender.

Misuse of Scripture

"I was accepted and celebrated for as long as I did what I was told. The acceptance ended the day I said no. I felt so used."

Unfortunately, in cultures of strong, spiritualized language with only two options available, the Bible is often used to drive the point home. When psychologist Donald E. Sloat, in his book *Growing Up Wholly and Holy,* describes a controlling church or family culture, he notes that "The unacceptable behaviors are defined, a motivational system of fear and guilt is established to ensure compliance, appropriate rewards and punishments are set up as reinforcers, and this entire structure is justified by Scripture."[26]

In healthy faith cultures, Scripture is used from start to finish as the foundation for following God; however, in controlling cultures, verses can be taken out of context to support the ideas or practices of that culture. In a healthy culture, Scripture comes first; in a controlling culture, their doctrine and practices come first, and the Bible is used to justify it all.

---

[26] Donald E. Sloat, *Growing Up Holy and Wholly* (Mandy Press, 2010) 65.

In his interaction with the enemy in the wilderness in Matthew 4, we see how Jesus responds to his accusations with verses from the Bible. Interestingly, the enemy also uses Scripture, but does so improperly, attempting to control Jesus by misquoting verses out of context.

> "If you are the Son of God," he said, "throw yourself down. For it is written: 'He will command his angels concerning you, and they will lift you up in their hands, so that you will not strike your foot against a stone.'" Jesus answered him, "It is also written: 'Do not put the Lord your God to the test.'"
> – Matthew 4:6-7

Jesus responded with "It is also written" to statements that *were also written*. While the enemy correctly quoted Scriptures that are always true, he did so unethically to gain dominion and control over another. This reflects the misuse of Scripture at the root of controlling Christianity as well.

Here, Jesus shows us that we can't take a verse out of its context and assume to automatically land on the correct conclusion, but we need to learn how to interpret the Bible using multiple verses in their correct contexts to get the intended meaning. Scripture is also clear that it is our adult responsibility to test what's been taught to us and not just accept it all without question (Acts 17:11-12). We ought to know the Bible so well that we can respond "It is also written" when someone is trying to justify giving us "a word from the Lord," such as the name of our future spouse, promises of miraculous yet conditional blessings, prophecies about personal suffering or assigned identities, specific instructions about our life choices, the next rapture date or any message "directly from God" that doesn't align with Scripture and respect our boundaries.

The list of evidence we have covered so far that reveals

high-control cultures—their tendency to place their leaders on pedestals where they can't be honestly evaluated, their demand for unquestioned obedience and loyalty, or their language that's only specific to them—can all be justified with Scripture. Our responsibility is to know the word of God so well that we can respond, "It is also written," when someone is trying to press us down by the misuse of Scripture, moving forward.

Another example where Jesus was faced with such attitudes is found in the story of the woman caught in adultery. It is one of the many moments where Jesus doesn't let Scriptures be used to hurt people. "The teachers of the law and the Pharisees brought in a woman caught in adultery. They made her stand before the group and said to Jesus, 'Teacher, this woman was caught in the act of adultery. In the Law Moses commanded us to stone such women. Now what do you say?'" (John 8:3–5).

The Pharisees in this scene weren't motivated by a desire for justice or restoration, or even to find the correct interpretation of the word of God. They were using this woman's story and Scripture to trap Jesus. The whole setup wasn't about her but about catching Jesus out.

"But Jesus bent down and started to write on the ground with his finger. When they kept on questioning him, he straightened up and said to them, 'Let any one of you who is without sin be the first to throw a stone at her'" (John 8:6-7). Jesus didn't debate theology. He turned the spotlight away from the woman and onto the hearts of her accusers. One by one, they left. "Woman, where are they? Has no one condemned you?' 'No one, sir,' she said. 'Then neither do I condemn you,' Jesus declared. 'Go now and leave your life of sin'" (John 8:10-11).

Jesus didn't deny the truth of her actions or the law, but he refused to shame her. He met her humanity with kindness and showed compassion that surpassed the wisdom and knowledge of all the religious leaders in this scene. He dismantled the entire structure of public condemnation and replaced it with an invitation to choose freedom.

He also showed that truth without love becomes judgment. Even in this story, where Scripture was present, love wasn't.

For those of you who have been made to feel like your worth depends on perfection or acceptance of others, this story is about you, too. Jesus is not like your accusers. He doesn't use Scripture as a weapon. He doesn't expose your vulnerabilities to humiliate you. Instead, he sees, defends and restores.

If you have ever felt like you have been dragged out into the open and judged by the people who claimed to speak for God, know this: Jesus does not stand with them. He stands beside you. He reminds you of your worth before calling you into wholeness.

He was and is nothing but good.

Chapter Seven

When Relationships Mirror the System

If you hold to my teaching, you are really my disciples.
Then you will know the truth,
and the truth will set you free.
– John 8:31-32

"I feel like I'm constantly being watched,
and doing something wrong."

"The church became the parent,
and I was afraid to grow up."

In high-control churches, you can usually witness unhealthy relationship patterns and imbalances of power, which often shape the dynamics between leaders and members of the faith community. These imbalances can go unnoticed at first but gradually foster an environment where individual boundaries are blurred, and personal autonomy is compromised. The result is a system where the well-being of individuals is sacrificed in favor of maintaining loyalty to the system.

A dysfunctional family or relational dynamic in which the boundaries between individuals are weak, poorly defined, or nearly absent is often described as enmeshment. In such relationships, communication tends to be intense, personal autonomy is limited, and individuals have difficulty maintaining a distinct sense of self.

Keep the sliding scale in mind here as well. Some levels of enmeshment are more intense and harmful than others, and people react to this in different ways.

In enmeshed family systems, individuals are overly and inappropriately reliant on one another, leading to family members over-identifying with each other. For example, children from enmeshed families may struggle to see or recognize their own interests or values as distinct from their parents' interests, feeling pressured to follow in their parents' footsteps without the freedom to fully process who they are as individuals. Additionally, in dysfunctional, enmeshed systems, children may learn to fervently defend their parents, even when their approaches are harmful or abusive.

This will greatly affect how their identities form and whether they can develop a sense of self-worth outside of their families.

Most healthy families are loyal to one another and often share similar values. In enmeshed families, however, this loyalty and shared values require children to sacrifice their individual identity, autonomy, and self-esteem for the "greater good." In these families, believing the narratives presented is deemed more important than forming one's own, personal, and accurate opinions about how things truly are within the family. Adult children trying to break away from such systems often encounter extreme resistance, emotional abuse, manipulation, and shaming from other family members.[27]

Enmeshment is characterized by excessive emotional closeness and a lack of autonomy. Parents in these systems often create both spoken and unspoken rules that closely govern their children's behaviors and beliefs. Family members typically turn to each other for emotional support and solutions to problems, but not to "outsiders." Parents in these systems often place unreasonable burdens on their children, implying that they should feel ashamed when they express a desire or need for something for themselves. Children in these environments are frequently

---

[27] Lewis, Rhona. "What Is an Enmeshed Family?" *Healthline*, 2020, healthline.com.

praised for maintaining the family's status quo.[28]

Family enmeshment manifests as diluted or loose boundaries, where individuals become emotionally intertwined. In enmeshed families, parents often become overly controlling or intrusive in their children's lives, preventing them from developing a healthy sense of independence. The children may exist primarily to please or appease the parents.

Healthy boundaries in families create safety and reflect respect for everyone's unique needs, thoughts, and feelings. Healthy emotional boundaries provide a safe foundation for growing children to explore their belief systems, discover who they are, what they want in life, and how they want to live, free from manipulation or shaming. As children grow, these boundaries should gradually shift to allow for more autonomy and greater privacy, offering them space to develop their own beliefs, values, and identities. In healthy families, children are encouraged to become emotionally independent, separate from their families, pursue their own goals and dreams, and fully become themselves.

Healthy family systems include intimacy, support, and unconditional love that never compromise the well-being of any member. Members of the family do not assume responsibility for someone else's emotional well-being or growth. Manipulation and shaming of members do not occur.

If you reread this part, replacing "parents" with "leaders" and "children" with "members," you will get an idea of where I am headed with this. Many of our Christian communities today show signs of enmeshment and, by doing so, often unknowingly, support a lack of autonomy in their members. They rely heavily on submission and obedience, and fail to support people to truly individuate.

When Benjamin first came to counseling, he was a young

---

[28] "Enmeshed Family Characteristics." BRC Recovery, 2021, brcrecovery.com.

adult who had grown up as a pastor's kid and was now volunteering in his church's teams.

He came to talk to me because he was feeling unfulfilled, even though he was "living his dream life." He had exhausted all his other options available to him, like working harder, praying more, and having discussions with his parents, other church leaders and friends, and nothing had helped him feel any different. He was sure there was something fundamentally wrong with him when he first walked through the door.

For the first few weeks of counseling, he kept sharing how he couldn't understand his anxiety at all because everything had been amazing growing up, and he was doing exactly what he was called to do now. And I listened, and reassured him that we would keep looking for an answer to this question together.

As we worked together, I kept supporting him in thinking through his own thoughts, not those taught to him, and feeling through his own emotions, not those prescribed to him. The way I did this was not to plant ideas in his head, but to ask more questions when he said things like "I've always wondered about this one thing," or "There's a part of me that has this question."

I would then offer to listen to that part of him without judgment, and every week, he started sharing more of himself, and less of who he had learned he was supposed to be to gain the approval of those around him.

Over the following weeks, the tension in his life grew. He started noticing how his genuine thoughts and emotions were always a problem for someone around him, whether it be his parents, his leaders, or his peers. And each week, he came to counseling, where I let him be exactly who he was without any need to change him, and he started noticing how this never happened to him in his real life.

Then, in one of our sessions, I introduced the idea of enmeshment to him. I read through some examples of enmeshment out loud to him, and he nodded his head through everything he heard. I reminded him that it was okay for him to take his time with this concept, and he could tell me next time if he believed this was his actual experience. I reminded him that it was safe to disagree with me, and I wouldn't try changing his mind if he did.

He came back again a week later and asked if he could share his story with me again. I welcomed the idea, sat back in my chair, and listened. With tears in his eyes, he shared:

"This past week has been incredibly difficult. I've realized that I've never known life without blurred boundaries and enmeshed relationships. I can't remember a time in my life when someone taught me to know myself, appreciate who I am and support me in making my own decisions. It was never seen as important.

"When you asked me about my values and dreams the other week, I realized that no one else had ever asked me that question before. I'm still unsure how to answer that question.

"What I have always been taught is submission and obedience, and this overpowered everything else. It overpowered me. It's so hard to say this out loud, but my life hasn't been amazing after all. It isn't amazing now.

"I grew up under the leadership of my parents and continued living under the leadership of our community. I've always felt a bit anxious and sad, but I thought it just showed a lack of spiritual maturity in me. I thought I was doing the right thing by doing everything my leaders wanted me to do. I've tried so hard all my life to be everything they wanted me to be, and now I've realized I'm completely exhausted because of it.

"I don't know who I am. I don't know how to trust myself. I know people around me mean well, but they don't know what they're doing."

It is very possible that many have grown up in enmeshed families themselves, or they have learned only one accepted way to lead in enmeshed "faith families." We often fail to recognize something as harmful when it is familiar. Because of this, enmeshment can be seen as good, ethical, and godly, even though it usually does harm.

There are certain behaviors and thought patterns you can observe if you are unsure whether there are signs of enmeshment in your family or in your church relationships. Trust your own experience and examine your surroundings as honestly and accurately as possible. Pay attention to any hesitation, defensiveness, or guilt you may feel, and accept these emotions as part of your process.

The following examples are of leaders and members of churches, but can also be transferred to mean parents and children of enmeshed families.

Behaviors of a leader in an enmeshed system:

• You expect the ones you lead to follow the beliefs and values of your faith community (or your own), and you feel personally responsible to check if they do.
• You encourage them to keep staying in your faith community but discourage them from practicing their faith or serving elsewhere.
• You take it personally when the ones you lead fail in any way; your self-worth as a leader depends on how well they perform, and you believe their decisions are a reflection of you as a leader.
• Your life is centered around leading these people and making sure they follow everything you have set for them to follow.
• You believe you need to model good, Christian attitudes and behaviors, and the people you lead should follow how you live your life.
• You want to, and you believe you should, know everything about

the people you lead.

• You reward the ones who do what you believe they are supposed to do and correct the ones who don't.

• You have been taught to believe that leading this way is good and ethical.

Behaviors of a member in an enmeshed system:

• You don't have a strong sense of who you are as an individual.

• You believe thinking about your needs is selfish and therefore sinful, so you solely focus on what others need and respond to their expectations.

• You make sure that your goals are your leader's goals and that you are in line with what your leader wants from you.

• You feel guilty when you take space or express having needs of your own.

• You avoid conflict and struggle with saying no.

• You find it almost impossible to make decisions on your own, or name your core values that aren't your faith community's or your leader's values.

• You feel like you must solve the challenges other people around you face, and that you are individually responsible for any disagreements, conflicts or difficulties.[29]

It is important to note that just because a leadership style has been around for decades, it doesn't mean that an enmeshed Christian leadership approach is healthy or appropriate. This leadership style can disempower individuals, preventing them from fully maturing into the people they were created to be, and fosters dependence on the leaders to guide and care for them.

---

[29] Lewis, Rhona. "What Is an Enmeshed Family?"

Here's how enmeshment can change the way we interact with others and the world around us:

1. Blurred Boundaries

• Because enmeshment is a systemic pattern where personal boundaries are blurred or nonexistent, individual identity, thoughts, and emotions are often fused with those of the group or family.
• Autonomy is seen as a threat to the unity and purity of the group, and therefore something to stay away from.

2. Group Loyalty Over Individual Autonomy

• As enmeshed systems typically prioritize group harmony and reputation over personal agency and growth, people may feel like their worth is tied to how well they follow the rules, believe the doctrine, and serve the community.
• Questioning, challenging, or sharing feelings outside of the accepted ones may be seen as betrayal and rebellion, which often leads to suppression and spiritual bypassing.

3. Identity Fusion

• Individuals often merge their identity with the group, where what they believe, who they associate with, and how they live their lives are dictated by the beliefs of the faith community.
• They may experience difficulty recognizing their personal values, dreams or goals outside of those of the group.

4. Guilt and Emotional Dependence

• Because control is often maintained through fear, guilt, and shame, people learn to see any personal boundary as disobedience, wrong, and spiritually dangerous.
• Individuals may experience pressure to conform for relational security.

5. Surveillance and Confession Culture

• There's usually a culture of reporting on one another, sometimes including family members.
• This can lead to chronic self-surveillance and a lack of privacy.

We will discuss healthy identity, values, autonomy, and leadership later in the book. For now, it would be a good idea to examine whether some of your relationships show signs of enmeshment. It is important to listen to the thoughts and emotions that naturally surface within you and reflect on what you have learned about leading and being led.

Consider whether there is a part of you that feels uneasy about the intrusive nature of this leadership style, and start listening to that part. What are these thoughts and feelings telling you?

What Control Is Not

"I was so afraid when I started feeling accomplished and goal-oriented. Maybe I was becoming selfish and prideful."

After looking at how enmeshment can trap us in unhealthy

relationships, it's important to be clear about what control is not. Not every influence, boundary, or expectation is controlling. In healthy relationships, these coexist with respect for everyone's individuality; guidance is offered without coercion, and accountability is never one-sided. Recognizing the difference better helps us see where the relationships we've built support us, and where they have started limiting our freedom to be who we are.

Here are some points you can consider:

Leadership is not control. Healthy leadership serves people and helps them grow into their whole, authentic selves. It can look like drawing out people's gifts and talents and helping them step into their full potential. Control demands obedience, sometimes in subtle ways, and suppresses individuality and autonomy.

Discipleship is not control. Healthy discipleship is rooted in the Bible and supports growth by encouraging questions, modelling humility, and walking alongside people in their journey. Control expects conformity and punishes difference.

Spiritual authority is not control. Healthy spiritual authority is expressed in servant leadership and accountability to both Scripture and community. It guides rather than demands, encourages discernment rather than passive acceptance and welcomes questions rather than silences. Control twists this authority into power over others.

Teaching is not control. Healthy teaching is based on the contextual understanding of Scripture and invites curiosity. It equips people to think, discern, test, and apply truth for themselves freely. Control uses teaching as indoctrination, where questions are discouraged and a single way of seeing everything as a group is enforced.

Expectations are not control. Healthy expectations are

grounded in consent, and consent can only be given when expectations are communicated honestly and clearly. They also always leave room for choice. Control uses expectations as unspoken rules and demands for compliance through guilt and fear.

Accountability is not control. True accountability covers all levels and layers of leadership first and members second and is always freely chosen. Healthy accountability can only be built on accurate information about each individual's responsibilities and consent, given without any pressure. Control removes this choice and uses "accountability" more as a surveillance tool.

Protection is not control. Genuine protection safeguards every individual's dignity, personal boundaries and wellbeing. Control claims to "protect" while it actually restricts freedom and autonomy.

Order is not control. Healthy order creates peace and clarity through clear roles in ministry teams and every individual's responsibilities. Control enforces rigid uniformity and fear-based compliance.

Understanding what control is not can help us see the difference between care and manipulation more clearly. It shows us that not every expectation or rule is harmful, even though some are.

Dr. Alison Downie, in her research titled *Christian Shame and Religious Trauma,* speaks about the difficulties many often face when they start sharing about their painful experiences in these communities. As you read it through with intentionality, allow it to sink in that this is what abuse can also look like:

> Those speaking up within religious
> communities can expect the truth of their
> experience to be minimized or denied;

they can also expect to be shamed back into silence in countless ways. Their character and religious commitments may be questioned, with implied or outright accusations that if their faith were stronger, their prayer more devout, or their understanding more spiritually mature, they would not have the experiences they describe. They may be accused of disloyalty, of betraying and harming family, community, or the larger religious tradition in sinful ways. – Alison Downie[30]

Reading through Part One, you may have noticed that control can reach far beyond rules and expectations. You may have started being aware that it can shape our sense of self, choices, and the way we relate to God and others. As we now move into the next section, we'll look at what control forbids and how reclaiming identity and autonomy is possible, even in the face of pressure.

I also want you to know that if you have been wrongly accused and hurt in any Christian system of control, I believe you and support you.

---

[30] Downie, Alison. "Christian Shame and Religious Trauma," *Religions* 13, no. 10 (2022).

Part Two
Recognizing Control by
What It Forbids (And Freedom Allows)

Chapter Eight

Building a Healthy Inner House

Everyone then who hears these words of mine and does them will be like a wise man who built his house on the rock. And the rain fell, and the floods came, and the winds blew and beat on that house, but it did not fall, because it had been founded on the rock. And everyone who hears these words of mine and does not do them will be like a foolish man who built his house on the sand. And the rain fell, and the floods came, and the winds blew and beat against that house, and it fell, and great was the fall of it.
– Matthew 7:24-27)

"The culture I was a part of conditioned me into patterns of behavior and disciplines that weren't natural to me. I never would've naturally ended up practicing my faith this way. I have been encouraged and corrected in ways that started shutting down the honest connection with myself and how I naturally live out my faith. Being able to critically observe what was happening around me was stolen from me, and made me sick."

Now that we have named control and seen what it can look like, it's time we explore what control tries to take away from us. In this section, we will focus on identity, boundaries, beliefs and autonomy—some of the core parts of who we are. We'll look at how building these internal structures can help us reveal whether the community we are a part of allows us to be ourselves or limits or pressures us to fit its rules. This is a practical step in testing control's parameters. By strengthening our sense of self, we can begin to test the environment around us and see whether it supports our pursuit of freedom or continues to push us down.

The principle we are looking for is this: the culture where we can rebuild a healthy sense of self is most likely safe. A culture that punishes us for it is most likely unsafe. We'll look at these parameters using the house analogy, which came to my mind on one weekday morning in September of 2022, when I woke up to this thought: *People are like houses. The outside walls are the boundaries of our personalities and bodies, and the front door is there to keep unwanted guests outside. We are the ones who should always be able to decide how to decorate our houses, what to hang on our walls, and, most importantly, who to let in.*

I could picture these houses—some calm and clean, some chaotic and messy, some filled only with loved ones, and some with unwanted guests walking around.

The thought about the houses seemed a bit strange to me at first, but it started making more sense later that same day. I was in a session with Elise, who had lived most of her life with a spiritually abusive family member. We were talking about identity when she said, "I think I need to reinvent myself."

I thought about how that would be like rebuilding, and from that, I immediately saw the houses I had pictured that same morning. Without any prior experience, textbook theories, or a clear idea of exactly where I was going, I felt compelled to take my chances with the house analogy. I shared this idea with her and wondered if she wanted to draw the house she felt she resembled that day. I didn't think of it at the time, but many therapy modalities, like Dialectical Behavior Therapy, use the image of a house as a tool for reflecting one's inner world.[31] In this chapter,

---

[31] "DBT House Activity: Building a Strong Foundation for Emotional Well-Being," Grouport, grouporttherapy.com

I'll explain how I felt led to use this idea in sessions.

With Elise, we discussed how healthy houses stand on healthy soil built on our personal beliefs, values, morals and faith rooted in Scripture. How they have strong walls and a door that's opened from the inside for the ones we decide to invite in, and how the relationships we build can be tested against the health of our own house.

Elise and I worked on two pictures together: one to describe the condition of her house that day, and another to establish dreams and goals for the house she wanted to become. First, she intuitively drew a house with a leaking roof and weak, broken walls, where rain and wind could blow right in, along with one of her parents coming and going as they pleased. Then, she drew another house with a locked door, strong concrete walls, a solid roof, and plenty of windows allowing beautiful natural light to come in. Elise concluded that this particular session was one of the best ones we had done together so far.

Encouraged by her response, I decided to try this house drawing experience with many more of my clients, and they all came back with the same report: people seemed to love this strange thing.

Our Boundaries: The Walls of Our House

"I was always expected to listen to others
over what I felt was right."

Outside and inside walls define the shape of our house and, alongside our front door, create privacy and safety. The communities we are in may have not learned this very well yet and have taught us how we must always keep our door open to let anyone in to comment on how they think our house should be organized and arranged. This can be called "speaking into your life" or "bringing correction out of love and concern." In high-control communities, these comments often reflect the rules learned, and don't respect each person's uniqueness. Rebuilding our boundaries requires learning how to put up healthy walls and doors, not to shut people out entirely but to choose who to let in, when, and why.

In mental health, boundaries can be defined as our personal limits that determine what we are willing to accept and live with in relationships with others, and what we are not. We know where we end and someone else begins. Boundaries can be physical, emotional, or spiritual. They also draw the line between what is private and public in us. With boundaries comes the need for clear communication about what we value, what is important to us, and why.[32] These values are best when thought through with intentionality and built on Scripture.

In high-control environments, boundaries come from outside of us as lists of dos and don'ts. They are defined by someone else, an authority of some kind, and we are expected to conform, follow the rules, and wear them like an armor of safety. While religious rules do create walls around us, they are not the ones defined by ourselves.[33]

Boundaries of control often exist at two extremes. In high-control groups, staying within these limits means rigidly following the community's rules. These constraints can diminish our ability to individuate and grow in autonomy and personal agency. Healthy boundaries, on the other hand, give us *an innate understanding* of what is our responsibility and what is someone else's responsibility. We recognize that we are separate from others, and that their thoughts and emotions are theirs, not ours to change. We understand the difference between proper and ethical encouragement or persuasion and improper and unethical

---

[32] Henry Cloud, Boundaries (Zondervan, 2017), 31.
[33] Anderson, *When Religion Hurts You,* Kindle Edition, loc 124.

control and abuse.

Correction is an important part of discipleship, but it is distorted in high-control cultures. There, every "misstep" is measured against the norms, rules, and practices of the culture. They are not entirely biblical as they leave so much out and use the Bible to justify their structures.

To understand our boundaries more clearly, it can help to discuss what they are not:

- **Boundaries are not cutting people off because they disagree with us.** This is an unresolved wound response. When we cannot tolerate differences or if someone challenges our thinking, stopping all communication with them is not setting a boundary. Healthy boundaries can hold disagreement with dignity and respect. We can walk away from control and abuse, though, and recognizing the difference is key here.

- **Boundaries are not about controlling others.** A boundary is meant to define what *I* will or won't do, not what *you* must do.

- **Boundaries are not walls against vulnerability.** While walls keep everyone out, boundaries help us discern who and what we will safely allow in. Inflexible and absolute lines often reveal fear more than self-respect.

- **Boundaries are not the avoidance of responsibility.** Using "that's just my boundary" as an excuse to avoid accountability isn't a true boundary. Healthy boundaries clarify ownership: this is mine to carry, that is yours to carry.

- **Boundaries are not a rejection of connection.** Boundaries are not meant to push others away but to help create safer connections. If our boundaries only ever end in disconnection, we may be reenacting old wounds rather than building new patterns.

If you want, you can also practice testing your healthy boundaries by noticing how often your "no" is met with guilt, spiritual pressure, or exclusion. In healthy environments, your capacity to choose, reflect, and grow is honored without coercion. You can say no when a request compromises your emotional safety, personal convictions, time, or autonomy, even if it's framed as obedience or submission. Pay attention to whether your boundaries are respected without punishment or manipulation. If saying no feels dangerous or sinful, that may be a sign that the environment isn't respecting your full humanity. Healthy communities allow space for both yes and no, without fear.

Testing boundaries can also be as simple as expressing a viewpoint that doesn't fully align with the dominant theology of the group. Whether it's challenging a teaching on gender roles, salvation, or end times, notice how your viewpoint is received. Are you engaged in thoughtful conversation, or are you silenced? In a healthy environment, disagreements will be met with curiosity and respect, not spiritual gaslighting or abrupt disconnection.

You're also not obligated to share every part of your story with everyone who expects you to do so, especially if trust hasn't been built between the two of you. Try holding back during group confessions, accountability meetings, or one-on-one conversations. See how others respond when you say, "I'm not ready to talk about that yet." If your boundary is met with accusations of hiding sin or lacking transparency, it can be a red flag. Healthy spaces honor your right to disclose personal matters at your own pace, not under pressure.

In high-control environments, you may have been taught that all correction must be accepted without question. This book is not encouraging defensiveness or an unwillingness to reflect on your own behavior. Instead, healthy boundaries allow you to remain open to wise and respectful feedback while also protecting yourself from manipulation, shame, or inappropriate intrusion.

You can also take a break from serving or attending every meeting and observe what happens. When you prioritize rest, self-care, or mental health over performance or productivity, do people support your choice or question your commitment? High-control settings often equate constant activity with strong faith, which can push you toward burnout. In contrast, healthy communities view rest as an essential part of spiritual health, instead of a sign of weakness.

Healthy boundaries will keep you safe moving forward, because people with boundaries are not difficult to lead, but they are impossible to control.

Individuation: House Ownership

> "I used to constantly check with others
> to figure out how I should feel about everything
> that was happening to me."

Once the boundaries of our house are secure, with doors that lock and windows that close, we can begin the work of individuation: choosing how we want to live inside. Individuation is about discovering what truly belongs to us apart from what we may have been taught to inherit. It's a step away from enmeshment towards mutual, respectful relationships, and real stewardship of what's been given to us.

In high-control environments, we may have decorated every room with someone else's ideas, believing it was the only way to live a godly life. Now, with stronger boundaries in place, we're free to walk through each room, ask honest questions, clear out what no longer fits, and decide for ourselves what stays.

Individuation in psychology means the process of becoming fully and uniquely yourself, separate from the beliefs, expectations, roles, and identities others may have imposed on you. It is the unfolding of your beautifully created identity, and the shedding of inherited, unhelpful patterns, painful past learning and false selves. In short, it is becoming who you were truly created to be instead of continuing to be who you have been told to be. It can look like:

- Differentiating your own thoughts, emotions, values, and desires from those you were taught or expected to have. It takes time and honesty to recognize what's truly yours and what was passed down and internalized through the culture around you.

- Integrating the parts of yourself you have disowned or hidden to "belong" or feel safe. Learning to connect with these disowned parts is a key step in becoming whole. You deserve to show up fully as yourself, not just the version that made others comfortable.

- Reclaiming your internal authority, trusting your own experience, intuition, and inner compass. You don't have to always defer to outside voices or systems to know what's right for you. You can build that trust within yourself over time, through genuine reflection and practice, in connection with Scripture and God's leading.

- Identifying which beliefs were internalized through obligation, rather than authentic conviction. These old patterns can shape your choices in ways that now feel heavy or inauthentic. You have the right to question them.

- Relearning to say, "I believe," "I don't know," or "This matters to me" instead of "We believe" or "God says."

- Differentiating God's voice from the system and its people. This can take time, but it requires you to slow down, be honest, and make space for personal connection with God and individual study of Scripture. What does he want to teach you?

- Exploring your dreams and desires without guilt because finding child-like enjoyment again is key to better mental health.

- Building relationships that are rooted in truth. Healthy relationships make room for our differences and help build bridges rather than burn them.

- Learning to tolerate disagreement, disapproval and discomfort. It's okay if everyone doesn't agree with you. It's okay if someone disapproves. These reactions don't have to define you or derail your growth. You can feel discomfort and still stay in a relationship with people, listen to them, and honor them.

Poor individuation can lead to a number of issues, such as increased anxiety, depression, lack of self-awareness, low satisfaction with one's life, low self-worth, poor decision-making and self-doubt.[34] Through individuation, on the other hand, we learn to make autonomous choices and grow in confidence and self-compassion. Over time, this process can lead to a new level of wholeness.[35]

True individuation doesn't mean rejecting other people's voices entirely, but it does create a healthier balance. It means leaving enmeshed relationships where boundaries are blurred at best, and forming new ones built on mutual respect. Healthy individuation helps deepen relationships with both people and God. When we learn to discern our own personal convictions

---

[34] Evie Kins, Bart Soenens, & Wim Beyers, "Separation anxiety in families with emerging adults" *Journal of Family Psychology*, 27 (2013), 495-505.

[35] Evie Kins, Bart Soenens, & Wim Beyers, "When the separation–individuation process goes awry: Distinguishing between dysfunctional dependence and dysfunctional independence," *International Journal of Behavioral Development*, 37(1), 1–12.

from those we may have blindly accepted before, we can bring our whole, honest selves before him rather than the masked version shaped by fear of disapproval. We can also start letting people see us, sometimes for the first time.

Healthy individuation also builds bridges between "us" and "them," and we realize that those categories were never as clear or necessary as we once believed. We become more curious than defensive. Instead of needing others to come over to our side, we start meeting them where they are. Connection becomes more important than the need to be right.

In healthy cultures, the process of individuation is welcomed as a sign of maturity. When we begin to question our own old beliefs or set boundaries, healthy communities respond with curiosity and care. They honor the slow, often uncomfortable work of growth, even when it may lead us in new directions.

In contrast, high-control systems often treat individuation as a threat. Instead of support, they offer warnings. Instead of respect, they give distance or rejection. The message is clear: conformity means safety, and autonomy means betrayal. But the truth is, becoming fully yourself is not rebellion, and healthy faith always leaves room for nuance.

Our Hidden Beliefs: The Old Furniture

"If you are tired, it's a sign you aren't praying enough."

Once the walls of our house are secured and we've begun the process of individuation, the next step is furnishing the space. In this metaphor, our beliefs are the furniture: the ideas, values, and convictions we live with every day. Some of these were inherited, handed to us early on and put in place without question. Others we may have picked up because they "matched" the room at the time, even if they no longer fit.

Individuation invites us to walk through each room of our house, take an inventory, and ask, *Do I still want this here?* This is intentional work of rebuilding our belief system: keeping what serves us, letting go of what doesn't, and choosing what we want to bring in next. We will look at how to recognize these pieces, test whether they still serve us, and decide which to keep, adjust, or remove.

During one session with Luke, who was also experiencing depression and exhaustion, we looked at the picture he was drawing and the furniture that was in his house. He had already drawn a lounge chair and a bookcase that held meaning for him, and I suggested that maybe there was also a big, old dining table in there that wasn't his but kept telling him something.

After taking a deep, long breath, he responded, "Yes, it's my grandma's table. It has a sign on it that says, 'You always have to persevere and never give up.'"

This particular sentence, with its word choices of *always* and *never,* had started creating an immovable response in him that prevented him from recognizing and admitting when he was getting tired and needed a break. A part of him had followed this rule so faithfully that he was now absolutely exhausted.

Whenever he would fail to obey this command, he was flooded with intense feelings of guilt. Feeling guilty is a healthy emotion when we have done something wrong, but it can also surface whenever we fail to follow the rules we have internalized.

Guilt can become one of the reasons we fail to recognize the unhealthiness of these rules because following their commands would bring us momentary relief from it. That is why guilt is not a trustworthy compass for someone in a controlling environment.

With this built-in guilt, Luke realized that he had also made the mistake of redefining sin. Every time he had even sat down for a moment to catch his breath or pulled back from church service just for a day, he had felt guilty and concluded that he had sinned.

This was not true. He had only been experiencing natural, human emotions, yet the rules in him demanded perfection. He decided that he needed to stop looking at things through a black-and-white lens and invite some nuance into his beliefs. The permission he needed was to listen to his tiredness with kindness, to take breaks and vacations more often, and to do this before he was so tired that he couldn't do anything but rest.

With the many people I worked with, it became clear that the old furniture in each of their drawings told them how to think, feel, and behave—in other words, how to be perfect—to fit in and be accepted by those around them. The old furniture provided them with rules to follow and parameters to stay within, explaining how a good Christian should live.

They were all big and sturdy, leaving individuals no room to move. Around these beliefs, life became pretty stagnant and immovable. Oftentimes, a life under such rules is painted as a life of sacrifice. The restraint they offer is often described as the road to sanctification and obedience, rather than being recognized as the burden of legalism, which they truly are.[36]

Most of the beliefs people shared with me resided in the words of their family members, pastors, team leaders, or friends. Some had picked them up on their own through assumptions or interpretations. Either way, it became increasingly clear to both my clients and me that some of the old furniture needed to go, and that we had to start decluttering their houses together. The reason for this is quite simple: learned beliefs can keep us stuck in patterns that limit growth and prevent us from living authentically.

---

[36] Donald E. Sloat, *Growing Up Holy and Wholly* (Mandy Press, 2010), 67.

Testing the Rules: Decluttering

"In order for me to be a part of this organization,
I have to constantly do better."

These rules we hold close to our chests can sometimes be confused with God's voice in us. Sometimes, in our desire to follow him, we can start clinging to the rigid interpretations of our internal beliefs because they feel safe and certain. However, over time, our house can start getting too cluttered, and our own thinking can crowd out the living voice of God.

Letting go of rigid thinking doesn't mean abandoning the truth; rather, it means we welcome new, biblical ideas into our previous learning.

Isla had to wrestle with these questions when she wanted to work through her exhaustion in counseling. She realized during her therapy process that one of the stagnant rules she held onto was, "You always have to do what's asked of you." This is what she shared:

"I remember being asked to join this outreach overseas, and I immediately felt that I shouldn't go. I was already very tired and felt it would be too much for me. I promised to pray about it, and when I did, I felt that my initial feeling—that I shouldn't go— was confirmed by God. I spoke with my team leader about this, who then started persuading me to go. He said he believed it was God's will for me to join their team. Because of the rule that had been taught to me and that I had accepted—to always comply without question—I said yes. I thought I was being obedient to God.

"The outreach was traumatizing for me. I became completely exhausted and had to come home earlier than others. Even then, I blamed myself for not being able to do what God had for me. I thought I had done the right thing by saying yes to my leader.

"I'm only now realizing that I immediately knew I shouldn't go, and after I prayed, I felt even more that I should stay home, but I disregarded all that because of this rule I had decided to live by. I didn't believe I had heard God correctly the first time around because of this rule in me that was communicated through my leader as well."

Isla realized she had become exhausted because of the internalized beliefs, and especially the immovable interpretations that she had lived by. Without realizing it, she had adopted a way of thinking that didn't allow her any space to move. It was either/or for her. She needed quite some time to regroup and recover after this, but I am happy to say that she is doing great these days.

Romans 12:2 says, "Do not conform to the pattern of this world, but be transformed by the renewing of your mind. Then you will be able to test and approve what God's will is—his good, pleasing, and perfect will." Renewing our minds can look like listening to the way we think with curiosity and prayerfully bringing some nuance into the immovable areas of our minds, where necessary. We can practice staying open and welcoming about the things that surface in us, not push them away as automatically wrong.

Below are some examples of internalized, controlling beliefs some of my clients have recognized in their sessions and where they mistakenly thought this was God speaking. You can probably recognize the use of loaded language in many of these as well. You can take some time to consider what it would feel like to bring some permission, truth and nuance into these beliefs.

"When you're feeling tired, all you need to do is to pray more."
"God will provide for you if you just stay faithful."
"Your breakthrough will come if you serve more."
"You always have to say yes and be excited about it."

"If you stay in the will of God, meaning in this faith community, God will bless your life. If you disobey and leave, you will fall."
"If you're feeling angry, it's a sign of sin that you need to quickly repent from."

It can be quite easy to believe that it's God speaking when our own internalized beliefs are speaking; after all, they exist in us largely because of the messages of our faith communities. Some clients' leaders often claimed to speak for God, so anytime they heard their mind repeat things from their leaders, it was quite easy to believe it was God's voice.

Our own internal critical voice doesn't only create internal rules, but often also overflows onto others. The pressure we sense inside can become the way we feel around other people who are not behaving the way our Inner Critic tells us we—and they—should. This is where we may, again, misinterpret our own rules as God's voice and speak them as divine messages. We may start placing our own criticism on other people, believing it's godly to do so.

It's good to keep in mind that conviction never feels like condemnation or criticism. It would be helpful to check these feelings and see how they sit.

Decluttering our houses is taking responsibility for our own inner work. We don't need to disregard everything and throw out everything that's ever been placed inside, but we do need to take time to listen to what our beliefs keep telling us and see if they are entirely accurate. Discerning Scripture correctly will be of great help.

If you recognize having been in a high-control environment, you are probably familiar with the unspoken expectation to believe that your leaders always hear God correctly and clearly. You may have started to feel pressured to shut down anything that would naturally arise within you, and this can rupture your discernment. Healthy communities, in contrast, allow everyone to listen and weigh in. You can test control's parameters by decluttering your internal house and letting go of what no longer serves you.

The Rooms of Our House: Parts of Our Personality

"Personality: individual's unique adjustments to life,
including major traits, interests, drives, values,
self-concept, abilities, and emotional patterns."
– American Psychological Association, Dictionary[37]

Houses have sections or rooms with different functions. Our inner life works similarly: we have different "parts" of ourselves that are all shaped by our histories, learned beliefs and natural temperaments. Some of these rooms may have been overused, some neglected. Some may now look the way the people around us have always wanted them to look, even though we may feel uneasy in them.

Self-awareness can look like walking through each room, taking an honest inventory of what's in there and why, and letting each one return to its original design. Our goal is to resemble our Creator more, not our culture.

These inner aspects that think, feel, and behave in their own unique ways can be seen as parts of our personalities. You might notice a part of you that's confident and outspoken, and another part that feels small and insecure. There may be a part of you that's playful and carefree with close friends, and another that becomes hyper-responsible and serious in times of stress.

---

[37] "Personality." American Psychological Association, *APA Dictionary of Psychology*, 2018, dictionary.apa.org.

These parts often show up in the everyday tug-of-war inside our minds. You might hear one part saying, "I should be productive today," while another responds, "What if I mess it up?" One part may say, "Don't speak up in that meeting, you'll just sound stupid," while another insists, "But my ideas are good and could really help others."

There are different names for these parts that we can find in psychological literature, but all agree on one thing: they exist within all of us, being parts of a whole, and there are no bad parts.

Our personality can be understood through what psychiatrist Eric Berne called ego states: Parent, Adult, and Child (written with capitals to avoid confusion with actual parents, adults, or children). These three parts are recognized as having different patterns of thinking, feeling, and behaving, and they can take control whenever we aren't aware of the ego state shifts we experience throughout the day. The more self-aware we become, the better we can use that awareness to make choices aligned with our values and faith, rather than our past.[38]

The ego state in us that can scan our environments objectively, ask questions, collect evidence, and calculate real-life possibilities is referred to as the Adult. When our Adult state is active, we think, feel, and behave appropriately in the here and now.

With this part of us active, we are very aware of our internal dialogues and movements, and we can make choices based on our core values with more ease. We can think through things from multiple angles, educate ourselves freely, search for evidence and evaluate what's really happening in and around us. This is the logical part of us that often whispers wisdom in our ear when another part is taking over. This part in us can help lead us

---

[38] Eric Berne, *What Do You Say After You Say Hello?* (Corgi, 1975), Chapter 2, Apple Books.

even when another part is trying to take the wheel.

With the Adult part active in us, we can think our own thoughts, not the thoughts we have been told to think, and wrestle with our questions, hold tension, think critically, and come to our own conclusions.

The Parent ego state is where we think, feel, and behave like our parents or caregivers did when we were little. Parts of our Parent state are also learned from our cultures, faith environments, and other significant aspects of our lives.

This ego state is programmed and learned, and therefore can be explored, restructured, and relearned. The Nurturing Parent is the part of us that offers care, comfort, and protection. It draws from learned patterns of how we were cared for or how we imagine care should look. At its best, the Nurturing Parent provides warmth and encouragement that helps us and others grow in confidence. At its worst, it can become smothering and overbearing, creating dependence instead of fostering maturity.

The Parent ego's thinking, which often manifests as expectations and standards for behavior, filled with "shoulds" and "should nots," is referred to as the Critical Parent. This critical voice isn't entirely ours—it is a blend of messages and beliefs we have absorbed over time through strict expectations of religious doctrine, the immovable rules of childhood, or the pressures to meet certain standards.

Often, this Inner Critic's voice is born out of fear of failure, fear of rejection, or fear of not being loved or accepted. Our Critical Parent is trying to protect us from other people's judgment, shunning, and shame, but by doing so, can stop us from finding connection and safety in the here and now.

This part of us may be unaware of it, but it often uses shame as a tool to reinforce its harsh judgments and keep us in a cycle of self-doubt. Every perceived failure can be magnified and woven into a narrative of inadequacy, convincing us we are fundamentally flawed. This shame often spills over, as we become harsh and judgmental also toward other people who are different from us, think in ways that are "wrong," or engage in behaviors that aren't "holy."

And we all have such rules within us.

The part of us where we think, feel, and behave like we did when we were kids can be referred to as the Child. We are likely functioning in our Child ego state when we feel the need to gain the approval of others, or when we feel judged by them, guilty about our real or perceived mistakes, or not good enough for whatever reason. Child can also quickly feel the need to please others, comply, conform, and over-adapt, or when we read into what we believe others are saying about us and start behaving based on those assumptions. The Child state can also activate in us when we are challenged by someone, and we become defiant and refuse to admit being wrong.

The Child in us may feel unworthy of love or approval, if its natural sense of wonder, curiosity, and joy is overshadowed by the constant pressure to meet impossible standards. This inner voice can make our Child state feel like we are constantly disappointing someone or failing in different ways. This experience can leave us emotionally bruised and unable to trust ourselves. The Inner Critic's harsh words not only stifle the Child's freedom in us but also create a sense of powerlessness, as if we are unable to escape the relentless judgment and condemnation that reinforce feelings of insecurity and emotional isolation.

Over time, the structure around us can become internal. It can become who we believe we are; our inner voice, part of our identities, and the way we believe God speaks to us. The rules of our faith community no longer need to be spoken out; we know what they are, what we are allowed to say, think, feel, and question. We have also learned what will happen to us if we resist, take some space or leave entirely. We know what will happen to our relationships within the system, our future, even our "calling."

If we imagine our ego states as the rooms of our inner house, and the furniture as the beliefs each ego state holds, then each space has its own purpose and feeling. The Adult room is where clarity and wise decision-making live. The Parent rooms can either feel nurturing and compassionate, or critical and demanding, depending on the voices we have inherited or practiced. The Child rooms hold our spontaneity, creativity, and wonder, and also often, fear, vulnerability, and shame. In a healthy house, each room has a place and can be visited when needed, without one overpowering another. They are all furnished in ways that feel right and help the air flow.

Doing this inner work is like creating more space for the Adult room and softening the tone of the Inner Critic. This part can too often dominate the Parent rooms and steal space from compassion and kindness. It can sometimes fill the whole house with judgment that overflows to other people as well. At the same time, we can practice opening the door to the Child rooms, where we let playfulness and tenderness come out without fear. The more we practice this, the more these rooms can connect to one another, and our house starts feeling like a coherent, welcoming space rather than a fractured one.

Healthy environments encourage this sort of inner work. They create space for people to visit and build up all their rooms; to grow in Adult strength, to quiet the shaming voice of the Inner Critic, and to welcome Child's freedom and need for comfort.

Controlling systems, however, forbid this kind of work. They often insist we stay in certain rooms and not visit others. They expect our Child rooms to remain silent and compliant, and the Adult room to be small and unfurnished. They teach us to build a loud Critical Parent room and almost a non-existent Nurturing Parent room, where self-compassion and permission live. They expect us to accept furniture that doesn't feel like ours and keep believing in their norms even when we don't.

Sometimes, discomfort can surface when we do this kind of inner work. It's very natural if the Child in us feels guilty, or the Parent remains harsh, even after our Adult has recognized these patterns as unhelpful and untrue in the here and now. These feelings settle over time. The problem is not our emotions, it's what we've learned to believe about them.

The Manager of the House: Adult

In every household, someone needs to manage the day-to-day decisions: when to pay the bills, what to get from the grocery store, how to maintain the space and when to repair what's been broken. Within us, the Adult ego state accepts this role. As we rebuild our inner house, strengthening the Adult is like appointing a wise caretaker who ensures that all the rooms work together in the best way possible.

In healthy development, our thinking abilities mature alongside our emotional and relational selves. As children, we begin by absorbing the world largely through the lens of others: parents, teachers, and cultural norms. Over time, we learn to weigh these external influences against our own perceptions, experiences, and values. We start to individuate, to become a distinct, self-led whole person rather than an extension of our environment.

A key part of this process is the healthy development of the Adult. This part of us gathers facts, considers evidence, assesses reality and takes a minute to ask what's really happening in and around us before reacting from a purely emotional or scripted part of us. In healthy environments, the Adult ego state is given room to grow because asking questions, challenging patterns, being curious, and exploring one's own opinions and conclusions are encouraged and seen as important.

The reason why this part of us often remains underdeveloped in high-control cultures comes from a lack of resources and from external expectations. Members of high-control groups are routinely encouraged to only read and study materials that their leadership has deemed "safe" and denied access to the very information that would strengthen their Adult state. It is common for leadership to forbid reading outside perspectives on their views, or to warn that such material is "poison" or "spiritually dangerous." If any critical information about the group is encountered, members may be told not to believe it, even if it's well-documented and verifiable.

This creates an information bubble, in which the only "truth" available is sanctioned by the leaders of the community. This makes it harder for people to compare and analyze information and seek the truth over doctrine. Yet, as Steven Hassan states, "Analyzing information is vital to understanding undue influence."[39]

In these communities, critical thinking is usually labeled as rebellion and flagged as a character flaw and spiritual immaturity, meaning people can't use their Adult ego states without repercussions. In worst cases, the threat of thinking freely is also followed by eternal consequences, and members may be told they are grieving the Holy Spirit by their doubts and questions. People are bound by fear and shame. Even so, it is more than possible to start studying and gathering relevant information from a wide variety of credible sources, even if it may feel scary at first.

Strengthening the Adult part can start when we give it regular opportunities to work. Our thinking abilities grow through

---

[39] Steven Hassan, Dissertation, 57.

deliberate practice. We would need to intentionally expand our access to information and perspectives that differ from the ones we have been taught to never question and reconsider the belief that learning will cause us to turn away from God. Critical thinking skills only grow through practice.

When we start being serious about learning, we will try understanding differing thoughts and views by searching for information that would prove their argument rather than disprove it. This way, our learning is no longer about protecting our fragile self-image but about engaging with reality and truth, even when it challenges us.

Strengthening the Adult is not about replacing one unquestioned authority with another. Rather, it is about the capacity to weigh evidence, hold complexity and tension, admit when we don't know something, and make decisions that align with both reality and our values and personal faith.

This may feel risky at first for those who have been taught that anything but submitting to leadership is dangerous and sinful. The emotions that may surface in the learning process speak more about the rules learned and the Child state panicking without a strong, internal leader than it does about the truth of the situation.

Developing our Adult thinking doesn't mean rejecting all authority or refusing all guidance moving forward. Many people leaving high-control communities fear swinging to the opposite extreme, where they trust no one, resist all leadership, or treat every opinion as suspicious. Healthy adulthood means we can still seek out experts, mentors, and communities we trust, because we have evaluated their values and ways they lead, but we engage with them from a position of choice rather than blind obedience. We listen, consider, and decide what to take on board, knowing that the final responsibility for our decisions rests with us.

Our biblical discernment is tied to a strong Adult functioning. This is where our minds are clear. We don't listen to someone just because they claim their message comes straight from God. The Bible works as our compass and how we trust ourselves in finding the truth over deception is key.

Here, we need whistleblowers who use their Adult states to expose the lies hidden in these beliefs. We need more people who build healthy houses grounded in biblical truth.

Growing in this more grounded state can also transform our relationship with God. We can learn to relate to him boldly and directly, and bring all our questions, thoughts and emotions honestly before him. We can become better at weighing the teachings we hear in light of both Scripture and our lived reality. We can learn to dialogue with him better and not expect our faith to be a one-way command chain anymore. Our Adult state can help us move from a fearful, rule-based obedience to a trusting, authentic relationship built on genuine conviction.

When a healthy Adult is present, the whole house is in better order and becomes livable. The foundation is secure, the walls are strong, all the rooms are checked for clutter and acknowledged for their functions, and the style is uniquely ours. From here, we can welcome others into a space that is safe and authentic.

Living in All the Rooms: Authenticity

"I've burned out from people pleasing,
and doing things I don't want to do."

Authenticity in our inner house means being able to move freely through every room without shame. In some houses, only some rooms are considered "acceptable" to enter or show to others. To practice living authentically, we want to open every door and make space for all parts of ourselves—even the ones that the culture around us has deemed sinful or selfish.

Grace practiced this during therapy. She came in for her first appointment feeling very confused. She had been working for a church for a few years, trying hard to do everything right. For a long time, she had been diligent about how she used her time both at work and outside of it. She had filled her quiet moments with reading the Bible, praying, and learning about faith. These are all good practices, but still, she seemed to be stuck in her confusion.

I started leading her to explore her authentic feelings and thoughts rather than the ones she had been taught. We looked at her personal values and natural gifts in search of who she was really created to be. During one of our sessions, she put her head down and finally admitted to me and to herself that she was, in fact, very tired.

"Have you shared this with God in your prayers?" I asked. She looked at me, a bit startled for a second, then laughed a little. "No, no, I haven't," she responded quietly.

Grace had been trying to cover up her creeping exhaustion by doing everything "right," by trying to be perfect, not herself. For a few years, she had been surrounded by a Christian culture that had told her to persevere. They had told her in many different ways that if she didn't feel victorious or hear God speaking to her all the time, it was because she didn't have enough faith, didn't pray enough, didn't have a truly surrendered heart, or didn't practice obedience.

Again, it all came down to her and her efforts if she were to have her breakthrough, so she had started trying harder to measure up. All this advice was now stored in her own Parent ego state, stealing all the air from the Child in her, restricting her Adult functioning.

She didn't know this at the time, but she had used a wide variety of spiritual activities, such as Bible reading and prayer, to shut down her emotions and thoughts—practicing spiritual bypassing and religious perfectionism instead of vulnerability and honesty. In this session, I asked her if she would be willing to give it all up for a week and just sit with God, bringing him everything she was feeling in her heart.

I suggested that she try sharing her most vulnerable emotions and thoughts with God. I encouraged her to attempt this for a week, knowing she could always pick her efforts back up again if nothing changed for her.

Grace came back for another session two weeks later. She told me how she had taken a break from work and during that time, she hadn't done anything "spiritual" but had just lain in her bed, feeling through what all the busyness had covered up. She shared she had noticed guilt and shame surface, extreme exhaustion in her whole body, and grief that made her weep every day. Even though this had brought her new levels of discomfort, it was also uncovering her authentic emotions and how she was truly doing underneath trying hard to be perfect.

When Grace stopped all the behaviors marked by religious perfectionism, she gave herself a chance to listen to how she was truly doing (not how she was told she should be doing). When she allowed herself to feel what she was feeling and honestly admit what she was thinking, she learned to know God as someone who wanted to meet her right where she was.

Healthy faith integrates our human emotions, natural desires, will, curiosity, and critical thinking, but in her environment, these were painted as sin and selfishness.

Learning to walk in authenticity means opening the doors of all the rooms and accepting all the parts that live in our house with kindness.

Doing the Inner Work

> "I used to always outsource all my inner work to God.
> I thought he was supposed to do all this, not me."

A functional house with reliable boundaries and a strong Adult manager can exist in a safe faith community. Problems only arise within controlling ones, where healthy development is seen as a threat to the system, but cloaked in spiritual language that can blur our discernment.

By practicing building a balanced internal life that's built on Scripture, you can test the parameters of your surroundings. Here are some quick, practical points you can use to check which ego state is activated in you:

- **Notice which room you're in:** Practice pausing more often and ask, *Am I speaking from my Adult, who is rooted in reality, my Critical Parent who carries all my learned beliefs, or my Child who's panicking right now?*
- **Soften the Inner Critic:** Challenge harsh inner messages with permission and nuance; practice replacing them with more compassionate, realistic perspectives.
- **Open the Child room's door:** Make space for rest, play, and creativity. Acknowledge any lingering fear or sadness with gentleness.
- **Connect the rooms:** Let the Adult in you learn new perspectives, comfort the Child, and set boundaries with the Inner Critic when needed.
- **Declutter regularly:** Notice furniture that you have uncritically accepted and decide if you still want to keep it.
- **Invite safe company:** Adult's job is to keep such unsafe

people out who keep hurting the Child and giving Inner Critic more ammunition. Practice spending time in communities and relationships that allow all your rooms to exist and support you in arranging them freely and with your personal convictions.

As we practice recognizing what freedom allows (and control forbids), it's natural to encounter waves of discomfort. There can be real sadness when we start to see how constant our Inner Critic's messages have been in its judgment, often echoing the voices we've become accustomed to hearing. The Child within us may have felt helpless or terrified for years and can now surface in moments of uncontrollable fear or anger.

It can be extremely distressing to realize that the very environments we have trusted to guide us did not support our growth in wholeness and authenticity. It can also feel overwhelming to recognize how much energy we have spent pleasing others, hiding parts of ourselves, or meeting impossible external and internal expectations. Our emotions are messengers and worth listening to. They are telling us the truth about our story that our reasoning may have tried to explain away.

Just as a house can crumble in harsh conditions, our inner world struggles when it's surrounded by control and criticism. In healthy environments, however, our house has space to be built well: the Adult can guide us with clarity, the Child can bring joy and spontaneity, and the Inner Critic is replaced with a warmer tone. Our inner house becomes secure and alive, rooted in Scripture and truth, open to growth, and ready to welcome life as it comes.

You have permission to build a healthy house, no matter where you are placed.

Chapter Nine

Don't Be You, Be Perfect

Above all else, guard your heart, for everything you do flows from it.
— Proverbs 4:23

"I've lost track of who I am."

Controlling environments rarely accept our wholeness but instead demand performance. Over time, we may not even notice the shift when a version of us driven by pressure and the need for approval takes the lead. In these cultures, *being you* often feels risky and *being perfect* becomes survival.

In this chapter, we'll explore a set of recognizable behavior patterns that many of us default to, often without realizing it. These patterns, known as **Drivers** in Transactional Analysis, act as unconscious defense mechanisms shaped by early experiences and reinforced by high-control environments.[40] The five core Drivers are: *Be Perfect, Please Others, Hurry Up, Be Strong,* and *Try Hard.* While we may carry traces of each, most people tend to operate primarily from one or two. These Drivers can feel like personality traits, but they are actually survival strategies—ways we've learned to stay safe, accepted, and in contact with those around us.[41] By letting go of the Driver-led versions of us, even a little, we can test if the environments we are in accept us as who we are, or if they only want our compliance.

Our Drivers develop at a young age as we learn which behaviors are approved or disapproved by the adults around us,

---

[40] Taibi Kahler. "Drivers: the key to the process of scripts." Transactional Analysis Bulletin 5, no. 3 (1975): 280-284.
[41] "Drivers in Transactional Analysis: 5 Key Drivers Explained." *Mindset Explained*, 2024, mindsetexplained.com.

as we adapt to their expectations. Our Driver behaviors are reinforced by the feedback, attention, encouragement, and corrections we receive, both verbal and non-verbal.

Even though Drivers are generally developed in childhood, they can also be reinforced in high-control cultures. Acceptance in these environments is always inherently conditional, regardless of the words spoken. In such contexts, Driver behaviors become essential for gaining a sense of acceptance in relationships. While our Drivers can be useful in a lot of ways and hold positive sides to them, they can also come at a cost, leading to stress and anxiety when we cannot fulfill their internalized messages.

Be Perfect. Individuals operating under this Driver tend to be precise and detail-oriented. They often speak in an even, steady tone and care deeply about how they and the things in their lives appear. Their internal dialogue or hidden beliefs may include thoughts like, "I must get everything right and be correct and wonderful in every way," "I must succeed in everything I do," or "If you want a job done properly, do it yourself."

The benefits of this Driver include being reliable, well-prepared, organized, and efficient. However, challenges arise from the high, often relentless standards they impose on themselves and others, leading them to fail to recognize when good is good enough. They tend to be highly critical of themselves, often without realizing it, and take others' criticism personally. This can result in difficulty delegating tasks and a persistent sense of worthlessness and dissatisfaction.

The Be Perfect Driver can create distance between individuals. Those who often function in this Driver may believe they are setting a positive example for those around them, yet they often end up distancing themselves from the authenticity of others. The Be Perfect Driver is religious perfectionism in action.

Since perfection is a moving target, nothing ever fully

satisfies people with the Be Perfect Driver, leaving them feeling quite empty.

Please Others. Individuals who operate under this Driver are often surrounded by people, smiling and engaging with them. Their beliefs may include thoughts like, "I must make people happy; I know I have done this when they acknowledge and praise me," "Other people's happiness is more important than mine," or "Only others can tell me when I have done well."

People with this Driver make excellent team members because they genuinely enjoy being around others and pleasing them, often without needing to be asked for help. They tend to be understanding, considerate, intuitive, and compassionate, maintaining harmony in groups.

On the other hand, they often avoid upsetting anyone and may hesitate to challenge ideas, even when they are incorrect. They might present their own thoughts as questions, lacking directness and assertiveness.

People with this Driver also take all criticism personally, even when it is constructive, and often try to read people's minds instead of asking questions. As a result, they may often feel overlooked, and their own needs frequently go unmet due to their difficulty in asking for what they need in an honest, direct way.

Hurry Up. Individuals who operate under this Driver often appear restless, fidgety, and even agitated. Their internal dialogue may include thoughts like, "So much to do, so little time," "Whatever I'm doing isn't being done quickly enough," or "Go faster."

People with the Hurry Up Driver walk fast, talk fast, and get straight to the point. They are busy, work hard, and accomplish a lot in a short amount of time. They thrive under deadlines and enjoy juggling multiple tasks at once, often preparing for them in a hurry.

Challenges arise when mistakes are made due to haste, and they may find themselves delaying until a deadline looms. This can lead to poor-quality work, impatience, and a tendency to rush from one thing to the next.

In their constant hurry, they often neglect to take the time to truly get to know the people around them, which can leave them feeling like outsiders.

Be Strong. Individuals who operate under this Driver often communicate in a matter-of-fact manner. Their beliefs may include thoughts like, "I must not cry or show any weakness," "I must help others but not myself," or "I don't need help."

They remain calm under pressure and feel energized when coping with crises, often thinking logically when others panic. They come across as even-tempered, firm, fair, reliable, and steady. However, they can also appear monotone and stoic, hating to admit any weakness, and to them, failure to cope is a sign of weakness. Internally, they can be highly self-critical, and others may feel uncomfortable around them due to their lack of emotional expression.

Because they withhold vulnerability and tenderness, they can be difficult to get to know. Deep down, they often fear being unlovable, leading them to avoid asking for help for fear of rejection. As a result, they may start isolating themselves from others and become withdrawn.

Try Hard. Individuals operating under this Driver often use phrases like "difficult," "can't think," and "try." Their internal beliefs may include thoughts such as, "I can't refuse requests; I must at least try," "I must improve and always get better," or "Wherever I am isn't good enough."

They approach tasks with enthusiasm, and their energy peaks when there is something new for them to do. They are often the ones who get things off the ground, and their enthusiasm can make them quite popular. They excel at problem-solving, see exciting new possibilities, and pay attention to all aspects of a task.

They also tend to be more committed to the act of trying than to succeeding, often leaving things unfinished once their initial interest wears off. They may struggle to complete even their own sentences and sometimes focus on irrelevant details when communicating, which can confuse those around them.

Mundane aspects of their work can be particularly challenging to them. They often create tasks that feel impossibly large and set unrealistic schedules, fixating on trivial details that don't help them finish their work. This self-sabotaging behavior can leave others puzzled about their actions, and they may frequently feel like they can never reach their desired goals.[42]

The underlying messages of these Drivers can sound like quiet internal commands, often disguised as virtues. They may whisper things like, "Don't be who you really are; just be perfect, keep trying hard, and please others," or "Don't feel how you truly feel; just stay strong for others and keep going faster." These messages are powerful because they are so often repeated and rarely challenged. As long as we accept them without question, they can shape how we relate to ourselves, God and others.

Each Driver serves a protective function, but without nuance and permission to explore beyond their rules, we can become trapped in conditional ways of being. When we operate solely from our Drivers, we may appear successful or composed on the outside, but internally, we often sacrifice authenticity, vulnerability, emotional closeness, and the very human need for unconditional acceptance.

---

[42] "What Are Your Drivers?" *The Link Centre*, thelinkcentre.co.uk

In healthy faith communities, we don't need to live from our Drivers to belong. High-control cultures, however, often reward the Driver-led version of us; the person who hides their needs, works beyond their limits, and suppresses their emotions. Over time, this can start feeling like the only self that is safe to show to others.

Scripture reminds us that God's grace is always enough, and his love is not conditional on our efforts. A healthy culture rests on this truth and intentionally creates space for honesty.

It Is Written

"I have to be on all the time.
I can never find rest."

Our Drivers often influence not only how we feel about ourselves but also how we view others and the events and messages around us. These internal patterns can become lenses through which we perceive the world, even including how we engage with Scripture.

When a particular Driver is active in us, it can color the way we read certain Bible verses. This can lead us to interpret them in ways that align with our internal beliefs or fears, rather than the text's broader context or intent.

This means that two people can read the same passage and walk away with very different feelings or takeaways, because they are reading it through different psychological filters. For instance, someone with a strong Be Perfect Driver might read a verse about holiness and feel pressure to never fail, while another person with a Try Hard Driver might read it as a call to exhaust themselves in spiritual effort.

This is all very human. We have all had moments where we approached Scripture through the lens of our inner narratives rather than from a place of grace and relationship with God.

Below are some Bible verses, each paired with a Driver. As you read through them, take a moment to notice your internal response. Consider how that specific Driver might shape or distort the way the verse lands in your heart. What would it feel like to read it through the lens of grace instead?

Be Perfect

Finally, brothers and sisters, whatever is true,
whatever is noble, whatever is right, whatever is pure,
whatever is lovely, whatever is admirable—if
anything is excellent or praiseworthy—think about such things.
— Philippians 4:8

Please Others

Let us not become weary in doing good,
for at the right time we will reap a harvest
if we do not give up.
— Galatians 6:9

<u>Hurry Up</u>

Do you not know that in a race all the runners run,
but only one gets the prize?
Run in such a way as to get the prize.
— 1 Corinthians 9:24

<u>Be Strong</u>

But as for you, be strong and do not give up,
for your work will be rewarded.
— 2 Chronicles 15:7

<u>Try Hard</u>

For this very reason, make every effort
to add to your faith goodness;
and to goodness, add knowledge;
and to knowledge, self-control;
and to self-control, perseverance;
and to perseverance, godliness;
and to godliness, mutual affection;
and to mutual affection, love.
— 2 Peter 1:5-7

It Is Also Written

All these Drivers hold power over us as long as they are believed. While they may have once helped us stay in contact with those around us, they also often demand rigid, all-or-nothing behaviors that leave little room for the complexity of being human. Each Driver could benefit from nuance and permission to be imperfect. We can begin to soften their edges by adding some color to the black-and-white world they often create. We can begin to practice what it means to be authentic and whole, rather than perfect and wonderful.

Practicing this will also help you test how well the community you're in accepts you as yourself. By observing how people respond when you show up authentically, you can start to notice the difference between genuine connection and conditional acceptance.

<u>**Be Perfect**</u>
Permission:
"It's OK to be who I really am,
and let people see me."

Because it is also written:
*But because of his great love for us, God, who is rich in mercy,
made us alive with Christ even when
we were dead in transgressions—it is by grace you have been saved.*
– Ephesians 2:4-5

<u>Please Others</u>
Permission:
"It's OK to take space,
and prioritize my own wellbeing."

Because it is also written:
Am I now trying to win the approval of human beings,
or of God?
Or am I trying to please people?
If I were still trying to please people,
I would not be a servant of Christ.
– Galatians 1:10

<u>Hurry Up</u>
Permission:
"It's OK to take my time."

Because it is also written:
Return to your rest, my soul,
for the LORD has been good to you.
– Psalm 116:7

<u>**Be Strong**</u>
Permission:
"It's OK to ask for help and be open."

Because it is also written:
But he said to me, "My grace is sufficient for you,
for my power is made perfect in weakness."
Therefore I will boast all the more gladly
about my weaknesses,
so that Christ's power may rest on me.
— 2 Corinthians 12:9

<u>**Try Hard**</u>
Permission:
"It's OK to just get it done."

Because it is also written:
I can do all this through him
who gives me strength.
— Philippians 4:13

Chapter Ten

Restoring Agency and Self-Leadership

"I've stopped saying stuff to just say it.
Before, I always tried matching other people
instead of staying present in myself,
and just being me."

As we have discussed, one of the ways to see whether a culture is controlling is to ask: Does it allow us to explore who God created us to be, discern our own values, and take responsibility for our choices, or does it insist that our beliefs and decisions are dictated by others? In high-control communities, questions like "Who am I?" or "What's important to me personally?" are often discouraged if they don't pressure people to land on answers the culture has deemed okay. Anything outside of these parameters is often seen as disobedience.

Healthy faith communities encourage us to grow in wisdom, exercise discernment, and live faithfully according to the gifts and convictions God has given us. This chapter invites you to continue to use these questions as a lens to test whether the culture you are in supports your growth in personal agency.

In psychology, agency means a person's ability to initiate and decide on their own actions, and being empowered to take charge of their own lives. It is both a mindset and a skillset.

When our worth is tied to compliance, we can start to doubt our worth apart from the role we play or the image we maintain in the system. Rebuilding a healthy sense of agency is essential for healthy living because without a strong sense of self-leadership, we will remain vulnerable to outside control.

In this chapter, we will explore the process of rebuilding agency through the lens of these three core elements: **values, autonomy, and self-leadership.** These foundational aspects have been essential to many individuals in their recovery after years of control. While there are certainly other aspects to consider, I won't be able to cover all of them in this chapter. I encourage you to continue learning about these topics in ways that work best for you.

Core values. In a controlling culture, our values often become blurred with those of our faith community's, so much so that we can't often tell them apart. We may not recognize what is uniquely ours as a personal gift from our Creator and what has been instilled in us through the uncritical acceptance of teachings we have received.

Our personal core values are the moral imperatives we are unwilling to compromise on and represent beliefs that hold deep personal significance to us. For example, they may include family, community, dignity, integrity, honesty, respect, wellbeing, health, and spirituality.[43] When we remain true to our core values, both personally and professionally, we stay true to ourselves and who we are.[44] In doing so, we create a life and build relationships that reflect our genuine self rather than conforming to someone else's expectations.

According to a study conducted by Moniek Thunnissen and Marian Timmermans, burnout can result from a chronic mismatch between an individual's values and the values of their workplace (or church). The issue lies in the rigid template used to interpret them and the narrow way in which they are applied in

[43] Guillemin, Michel, and Robin Nicholas. "Core Values at Work—Essential Elements of a Healthy Workplace." *International Journal of Environmental Research and Public Health* 19 (2022): 12505.
[44] Paliliunas, Dana. "Values: A Core Guiding Principle for Behavior-Analytic Intervention and Research." *Behavior Analysis in Practice* 15 (2021): 115–125.

practice.[45]

An important step in identifying your core values and comparing them with those of your faith community is examining how they are practiced in everyday life. As discussed in Chapter Five, language matters. On paper, you may agree with your community's values, but there may be a disconnect between what is stated and how they are lived out. Keep this in mind as you reflect on this question.

For example, when Sarah realized that she had been working around 70 hours each week for months, she had been living according to the values of service and faithfulness. Both of these were good, but the way they were being implemented was unhealthy, and they were trampling on some of her other values, such as fairness and balance. This was something Sarah could no longer accept once she started seeing the situation clearly.

These are some important points you may want to consider:

• **Knowing our values is a biblical invitation to personal discernment.** Scripture repeatedly encourages us to test everything, hold onto what is good (1 Thessalonians 5:21), and come to our own convictions before God (Romans 14:5). Discovering our God-given values is a step towards real, honest spiritual maturity and responsibility.

• **Values offer us an internal compass.** When we are still unaware of our personal values, we may more easily swing between these two extremes: either holding on to external rules or rejecting all guidance. Personal values provide us with steady direction that isn't dependent on another person's approval or

---

[45] Thunnissen, Moniek, and Marian Timmermans. "Transactional Analysis and Burnout: For Individuals and Organizations." *Transactional Analysis Journal* 53, no. 4 (2023): 328–40.

outside influence.

• **We are invited to start distinguishing our personal values from inherited pressure.** Many beliefs we hold while we are still in a high-control environment are handed down to us, not freely chosen. Identifying which ones we genuinely believe in and which we now see as fear-based control tools will help us separate faith from indoctrination.

• **Values can prevent us from re-entering control.** When we know what we stand for, believe in, support, and are ready to fight for, we are less likely to be drawn back into another unhealthy structure disguised as "truth."

• **Knowing our values reduces inner conflict.** When our actions align with our values, we feel more at peace, even when others may disagree or disapprove. This helps reduce shame and people-pleasing patterns.

• **Values help us in building authentic relationships.** Shared values can become the foundation for healthy and equal relationships instead of shared rules.

• **Knowing our values encourages nuance and growth.** They are flexible enough to grow with our life experiences. Values don't demand perfection, but rather invite ongoing reflection and learning.

• **For example,** someone whose core value is faithfulness doesn't need to stop and pray about whether they should stay loyal to their spouse. It comes naturally, regardless of other people's opinions or external pressure. They remain committed because their actions align with their values and personal convictions. In the same way, I hold values like autonomy, integrity, honesty, safety, freedom, authenticity, healing and restoration, and responsibility and stewardship. I don't have to pray about these anymore – I know these values rest on what God has given me to steward well. Because of these convictions, it is impossible for me to ever again participate in a system that controls people.

Locus of control refers to our beliefs about what influences our lives and how much control we feel we have in our own behavior. When we have an *internal locus of control,* we believe our own actions, choices, and efforts directly affect what happens to us. In contrast, an *external locus of control* means we attribute outcomes to external forces, such as authority figures and the structures of our faith community. The rules we are taught in high-control environments place the locus of control outside of us, and diminish our ability to make choices that are truly ours.

When James first came to see me in Chapter Six, he had shown a high external locus of control for years by not booking his appointment, even though a part of him knew he needed additional support. By making the decision to seek counseling, he shifted the locus of control closer to himself.

When we have a strong internal locus of control, we tend to be more independent, less conforming and obedient, and therefore more problematic in controlling environments. We are also better at resisting social pressure to conform or obey only because we are expected to do so. This, of course, doesn't mean we refuse guidance simply for the sake of it, because that wouldn't come from a healthy value.

One of the first steps in bringing your locus of control closer to yourself is becoming clear about your personal core values and how you believe they should be lived out. If you are interested, this is what you can do:

1. As honestly as possible, write down what is important to you. Do your best to answer with integrity and clarity. There are no correct answers or things you should or should not say.
2. As honestly as possible, think about the times when you are your happiest, the most excited, and where life seems to be flowing freely through you. What are you

doing? Who is with you?

3. As honestly as possible, write down moments and achievements when you have felt proud of yourself. What did you accomplish?

4. From these answers, try to identify common themes. What is emerging as essential to you?

After this, write down a list of values that intuitively come up for you based on your answers. Reflect on how you believe they should be lived out in your life, and assess whether you are currently living according to your God-given core values or not. Think also of how they could all coexist in you, with all of them carrying significance.

Autonomy. On the opposite side of control lies autonomy, our human right to self-government. The environments we are in and the discipleship we receive can either support our autonomy (i.e., promote choice) or control our behavior (i.e., pressure us toward a specific outcome).

Autonomous people **make independent decisions based on their core values.** They have a strong internal locus of control and are not quickly swayed from their true selves or their God-given convictions under pressure. Autonomy is more than being independent and has nothing to do with rebellion. It is an **innate freedom** that allows people to act on their own behalf, stay true to themselves, and take charge of the lives they were created to live.

Research conducted by Edward L. Deci and Richard M. Ryan showed that supporting one's autonomy is generally associated with having more intrinsic motivation, experiencing less stress and tension, being more creative, having greater cognitive flexibility, becoming better at contextual learning, experiencing a more positive emotional tone in life, having higher self-esteem, being more trusting, showing greater persistence in behavior change, and experiencing better physical and psychological health.[46]

On the other hand, lack of autonomy has been linked to lower life satisfaction, apathy, cynicism, greater stress, burnout, anxiety and depression, feelings of anger, guilt, and fear, and a lack of purpose. Living under the pressure of control can strip away our autonomy, leading to a life of unfulfillment. Life can become a continuous effort to meet external expectations, while feeling that wanting something more or different is wrong, because we should only be happy and thankful for where we are.

In some faith cultures, the symptoms linked to a lack of autonomy are explained as our flesh or sinful nature trying to live selfishly, when in reality, the reasons are way more complex, and often far less spiritual, than that.

When we are connected with our values and living according to them as autonomous adults, our preferences, behaviors, needs, motivations, and faith in God are all better aligned. There is a lot less inner tension, if at all, but rather a permission to live a life that comes naturally to us.

If you place an autonomous person in a controlling environment, you will for sure witness quite a bit of tension. Autonomy does not mix with control, as they are on opposite sides of the same continuum. In controlling cultures, autonomy is often misinterpreted as defiance, problematic independence, or a lack of Christian character.

In reality, autonomous people are not as problematic as control paints them to be; in fact, they are often more motivated, creative, trusting, and persistent than those who merely respond to external expectations.

---

[46] Deci, Edward L. and Richard M. Ryan. "The support of autonomy and the control of behavior" *Journal of Personality and Social Psychology*, 53, no. 6 (1987): 1024.

Self-Leadership. People who are aware of, in touch with, and living according to their core values as autonomous adults make strong leaders in their own lives. We would grow in listening to God's guidance over pleasing any system, even when our decisions would go against the prevailing current. And we can't lead other people unless we can first lead ourselves.

In *Necessary Endings*, Dr. Henry Cloud emphasizes that great leaders are in touch with reality. They no longer deny dysfunction or remain wishful about things that may never come to pass but instead make brave decisions to end things and seasons that aren't going anywhere. They are brave to move forward, and make healthy changes, whenever necessary.[47]

In leading ourselves, we would naturally begin making decisions that align with our values and actively saying no to everything that clashes with them. Living according to our values is not going to be easy, because any meaningful, personal change comes with loss. We will discuss this more a bit later.

As strong leaders, we would also learn to choose our environments wisely. We would spend time getting to know the culture, making sure they don't lead through control, and asking questions to make informed decisions. We would be better equipped to choose communities where we naturally align with their broader values and practices of the group, instead of forcing ourselves to agree with everything because it is "the right thing to do."

We will likely start to notice that, with our inner leader in place, we will not only lead ourselves toward places that align with our values, but also lead ourselves away from and out of those that don't.

---

[47] Henry Cloud, *Necessary Endings: The Employees, Businesses, and Relationships That All of Us Have to Give Up in Order to Move Forward* (Harper Business, 1998), 74.

Healthy Leadership

"I started believing that I can't do anything right
without my leader."

Values, autonomy, and self-leadership can only flourish when people are treated as capable adults. When the leadership style slips into Parent ego state, the whole dynamic changes. The tone becomes supervisory, controlling, or corrective, even when it's well-intentioned. People under such leadership are no longer invited to think with personal discernment, but guided, pressured, or managed in ways that cross healthy boundaries.

Healthy faith doesn't require us to be spiritually parented. Instead, it calls us to grow, think, challenge, wrestle, and steward our own callings and walks with God. Understanding the difference between Parent-led and Adult-led leadership is one of the keys in building healthy faith communities. Here are some examples:

Parent-led Leadership:	Child state Response:
"God told me this, so you must listen to me."	"If I doubt them, I'll doubt God. I can't risk it."
"If you don't follow me, you are disobedient to God."	"If I disobey, I'll be punished by God."
"You are not a true Christian if you don't receive my message."	"I must do everything I can to prove that I am a true Christian."
"You need me to take care of you and your faith."	"I can't trust my own discernment."
"It's dangerous for you to make decisions on your own."	"If I make decisions without them, something bad will happen."

Under such Parent-led leadership, the Adult state will have difficulties growing. It can be very challenging to leave these dynamics, because the Child ego state in individuals doesn't grow in self-trust, but it grows in trusting others to tell them how to think, feel, and behave. Confusion is often a prevalent emotion alongside guilt, shame, and fear. In these cultures, the Adult state is painted as a sinful part, so people often try very hard to make this part go away.

Underdeveloped Adult ego state is a real injury, and part of the trauma inflicted on individuals in controlling environments.

Being under Parent-led leadership conditions people to silence their own voice and doubt themselves. This is not a personal weakness but a predictable outcome of an unhealthy system. It can create confusion where the logical, more grounded part, the Adult, will keep quietly asking questions about the rules around them, but is wrongly interpreted as a problem. The control many individuals have received has labeled this part as rebellious and divisive. It's too independent and accuses others and gets offended for nothing. It doesn't know how to just give these things to God and not worry about them and keep trusting the leaders who always know what to do. This kind of language creates confusion because it's not truthful.

For many, the healing process often includes doing some inner work where they intentionally build a healthy identity "house" in environments where it's safe to do so. Many find it helpful, even though painful sometimes, to continue to evaluate their own inherited and now stagnant beliefs with curiosity and bring in a bit more permission and nuance to their dualistic world where needed.

Wholeness can also grow as people practice asking: "Is this true? Is this fair? Is this biblical?" and counter their own Critical Parent messages with kindness, saying, "I don't have to be perfect to have intrinsic worth. Asking questions is a sign of maturity, not disobedience. It's simply not true that I am always wrong and my leaders are always right."

Restoring agency after Adult wounds often means practicing living in true authenticity, where all the rooms of their identity house are seen as valuable. It's learning to live in wholeness, where all the personality parts have a role, led by a healthy Adult. While others can offer support, only the individual can build their own inner house from within.

Each person is invited to carry the responsibility of this work and not give it to God, church leaders, or parents. People's emotional, spiritual, and psychological growth cannot be handed over to someone else. All these aspects grow as each individual takes ownership of becoming the whole human being they were originally designed and created to be. Though many may have tried to silence their Adult self under pressure, it never truly goes away. It may be quiet, but it's there. This part will eventually be their ticket out of control.

In contrast, here are some things to consider in recognizing when someone is leading from their Adult ego state:

- They are grounded in reality. They acknowledge both the joys and struggles of faith without denial or exaggeration. They share openly about their current challenges of growth, not just "before and after" stories. They don't create rules and social norms and then search for verses to justify them.
- They encourage critical thinking and model how to do it. They are open to learning about a wide variety of topics from multiple, credible sources rather than just their own. They invite questions and exploration of Scripture.
- Their communication is transparent. They say what they mean without hidden agendas, spiritually loaded language, or manipulation.
- They practice healthy discernment and listen to others'

feedback and input. They treat everyone as their equals in worth and dignity, never as subordinates.

- They take responsibility. They admit to their mistakes, apologize, and accept fair consequences for their actions.
- They show a balanced emotional tone. They don't swing between over-controlling their emotions and over-indulging in them, but respond appropriately in the here and now.
- They facilitate the growth of everyone's autonomy. They trust people to make their own decisions wisely. They honor everyone's personal values.
- They are open for correction and healthy discipleship. They voluntarily stay accountable to the people around them and welcome outside oversight. They don't place themselves above other leaders, the community, or Scripture.
- They hold their own boundaries. They are neither enmeshed nor distant from the people they lead, but clear and fair about what's public and private.
- They use Scripture responsibly. They apply it wisely in its correct context, not as a weapon to shame or silence.

Under Adult-led leadership, people typically feel respected and trusted. They learn to trust themselves and learn to think for themselves. They notice that honesty is valued over blind compliance. Internally, many often feel a calm confidence and genuine engagement with others. They would safely be able to build a healthy identity house and notice others doing the same. They would experience very little internal conflict, no confusion, and a strong sense of clarity.

This leadership style would help members to stay and strengthen their own Adult state, where they are responsible for their own learning, growth, and discernment. Here, every individual can keep healing from their past wounds.

Here are some examples of what Adult leadership style can sound like, and the ego state that is invited in those being led:

Adult Leadership:	Adult Response:
"Here are some resources and different perspectives. I encourage you to read and decide what you believe."	"I can take this information, consider it, and come to my own understanding and use my discernment."
"Let's explore your questions together and see what Scripture, history, and experience say."	"I can voice my doubts without shame, knowing that seeking is part of spiritual maturity."
"Your decisions are your own. I may share my perspective, but I respect your responsibility in this."	"I can set boundaries and listen to others without losing my sense of agency."

It is good to keep in mind that healthy submission can only happen under healthy leadership. Submission in this context is not blind obedience, but a conscious, voluntary choice to trust the guidance of a leader who demonstrates integrity and fairness. Without such leadership, submission can become manipulative or damaging.

Part Two has shown us how control tries to forbid the very things that make us whole: our ability to think critically, our freedom to choose, and our boundaries. When these are honored, our identities can grow strong and our faith gets to mature. When they are denied, we start to shrink to fit a system rather than live as who we are.

Losing some of these essentials affects more than just how we think and behave. In the next section, we will look at the impact of control on our hearts, exploring how these pressures can leave real bruising in us. From here, we turn to the impact of control itself: how it can create patterns of fear, shame and injury that we now recognize as trauma.

Part Three
Recognizing Control by Its Impact

Chapter Eleven

Religious Trauma

"The scariest and the most freeing thing
I learned in therapy was that I was traumatized by control."

Often, when we are still involved in a controlling culture, we may not notice what's happening in and around us. We often learn to believe the narratives where any discomfort we may feel is all our fault, and we keep searching for answers from within. We may also use a wide variety of survival mechanisms, such as people-pleasing and perfectionism, which can cover the real shape of our hearts, and can make it hard to recognize control for what it is.

We can also practice recognizing control through its impact on us. This is where the term *religious trauma* comes into the picture. It explains the wounding some individuals experience in controlling faith environments.

You can think of trauma as the aftermath of a car crash. If five people are in the same car during impact, not all of them would leave the scene with exactly similar injuries. Depending on where they were sitting, if they were wearing seat belts, how healthy they were at the time of the accident, and where the collision happened exactly, they would all suffer from different kinds of physical and psychological harm.

Similarly, in the context of religious, emotional and spiritual trauma, not everyone reacts in the exact same way having been a part of the same high-control culture. The culture may very well be controlling; some just remain less affected by its practices, while others suffer. And if even one suffers, this needs to matter to the whole community.

In this section, we will explore the impact of control on our emotions, thoughts, and nervous systems by naming the wounds correctly.

These wounds in high-control contexts don't always come from one major event. They can build gradually, and are often shaped by discreet, repeated interactions, subtle power dynamics, and systems we move through over time. Hillary McBride explains in her book *Holy Hurt* how these repeated experiences, even if they don't seem catastrophic in isolation, can create lasting emotional scars, especially when there is little time or recognition for recovery or healing in between.

In some cases, the accumulation of these events can lead to a more pervasive sense of fear, anxiety, or helplessness, which compounds the trauma over time. These aren't always easy to name, especially when the system itself teaches us to disconnect from our own internal cues.[48]

The nervous system plays a crucial role in how people experience and process trauma. When individuals encounter a traumatic event, their body's natural survival mechanisms kick in. The autonomic nervous system activates and triggers a fight, flight, fawn, or freeze response, the body's primary responses when people are faced with an inescapable or overwhelming

---

[48] Hillary L. McBride, *Holy Hurt: Understanding Spiritual Trauma and the Process of Healing* (Brazos Press, 2025).

threat. These reactions are ingrained in us as human beings, and they can be lifesaving in dangerous situations.[49]

The fight response involves a surge of adrenaline and other stress hormones, preparing the body to confront or overpower the threat. This response is often associated with anger or aggression, where the individual may feel the need to protect themselves or others.

The flight response, on the other hand, triggers a rush of energy that prepares the body to escape the danger. This can manifest as a strong urge to run away, hide, or find a way to avoid the threat altogether.

The fawn response involves people-pleasing behaviors and attempting to appease those perceived as threats, often to avoid conflict or further harm. This can lead to individuals sacrificing their own needs or boundaries to maintain a sense of safety.

The freeze response occurs when the body becomes immobilized or "shuts down" in the face of overwhelming fear. This can feel like a complete dissociation from the body or the situation, as if the person is frozen in time, unable to move or act.

While these responses can be protective in the short term, when trauma is unresolved or repeated, these responses can become overactive or chronic, which can cause the nervous system to stay in a heightened state of alert. This can leave individuals feeling anxious, hypervigilant, or emotionally numb long after the event has passed.

Gabor Maté explains trauma as "an inner injury, a lasting rupture or split within the self due to difficult or hurtful events. By this definition, trauma is primarily what happens within someone as a result of the difficult or hurtful events that befall

---

[49] Peter A. Levine, Waking the Tiger: Healing Trauma: The Innate Capacity to Transform Overwhelming Experiences (North Atlantic Books, 1997), 16.

them; it is not the events themselves. Trauma is not what happens *to* you but what happens *inside* you." He also adds that, "An event is traumatizing, or retraumatizing, only if it renders one *diminished*, which is to say psychically (or physically) *more limited* than before in a way that persists."

Therefore, trauma may very well be prevalent, present, and true in a person's life, if the events around them have left them feeling limited or constricted, or have diminished their capacity to feel, think or assert themselves freely, or haven't allowed them to experience their own suffering without it completely overwhelming them or being able to witness it with compassion.[50]

Healing from trauma, then, is not just about dealing with the memories of the event itself but about helping the nervous system return to a regulated state where it feels safe and grounded again. Bessel van der Kolk, in his book *The Body Keeps the Score*, highlights that trauma's impact is stored in the body, and the path to healing requires restoring balance within the body and mind.[51]

Just as trauma in any context overwhelms a person's ability to cope, religious trauma follows the same patterns in the body and mind. The setting may be spiritual, but the impact remains the same. Fear, shame, chronic stress, and loss of agency register in the nervous system in identical ways regardless of where they originate.

This means that healing from religious harm is not a separate category of care but part of the broader work of trauma recovery. The same principles of safety, choice, compassion, and body-based regulation remain essential for people recovering from trauma, religious or otherwise.

Religious trauma is a term that is defined in slightly different ways by scholars and practitioners. For the purposes of

---

[50] Gabor Maté, *The Myth of Normal: Trauma, Illness, and Healing in a Toxic Culture* (Avery Publishing, 2022), Loc 24-25, Kindle.
[51] Bessel van der Kolk, *The Body Keeps the Score: Brain, Mind, and Body in the Healing of Trauma* (Penguin Books, 2014).

this book, we will use the definition developed by the Global Center for Religious Research, as it emphasizes both the psychological and spiritual impacts of high-control environments:

> Religious trauma results from an event, series
> of events, relationships, or circumstances
> within or connected to religious beliefs,
> practices, or structures that is experienced by
> an individual as overwhelming or disruptive
> and has lasting adverse effects on a person's
> physical, mental, social, emotional, or
> spiritual well-being.[52]

I understand if it feels difficult to connect how trauma like this could ever originate in a Christian church. What is so dangerous about them — they aren't life-threatening, after all.

The constant sense of danger, threat, and overwhelm our nervous systems can pick up in these environments often fly under the radar. But if we look at this a bit more closely, we may notice that:

Speaking up feels dangerous. Experiencing fear of being shunned, disciplined, corrected, or ignored can trigger the same alarm bells as physical danger, since belonging to a group is one of our core needs.

Expressing emotions feels dangerous. Experiencing fear of the loss of attachment with our family, friends, or community that we know would follow if we were completely honest about our internal struggles, can trigger our nervous system's fawn response, and keep it there for long periods of time without resolution.

Having doubts feels dangerous. And when these doubts are

---

52 "Percentage of U.S. Adults Suffering from Religious Trauma: A Sociological Study," *The Global Center for Religious Research,* gcrr.org.

expressed, we may be humiliated—often experienced as public, forced confessions—which can activate our body's threat response.

Setting boundaries feels dangerous. We may recognize an inability to say no, or we may feel bad when we inconvenience someone in any way.

Not being able to submit well feels dangerous. The fear of not being a good follower can signal constant danger to our system.

Others, or the life outside our group, feels dangerous. The demonization of other worldviews, callings, lifestyles, people, sermons, pastors and groups of faith can isolate us from the larger community around us and heighten our internalized fear.

Being you feels dangerous. All that naturally arises within you is often seen as wrong if it goes against the group's behavioral expectations. The self-monitoring, feeling of being constantly watched, and fear of eternal punishment can lead to chronic stress and overwhelming of the nervous system.

As Gabor Maté also explains, trauma separates people from their bodies. When the body signals constant threat and danger, even when it might not yet be consciously recognized, people begin to live in their heads, thoughts, and mind, instead of fully experiencing life as it comes.

The disconnection from the body can show up as perceived strengths, like being able to perform at a high level even when hungry, thirsty, stressed, or tired, without any awareness or registered need to pause, eat, or rest. For some, this disconnect can show up as not knowing when to stop eating or drinking, as the "enough" signal does not get through. It can also show up as unawareness of emotions, flatness, numbness or the inability to recognize feelings as they arise. It can lead to pushing through and forcing one's way forward.[53]

For those who have spent years inside a controlling or performance-based system, it is important to understand that the injury doesn't always appear immediately. Its effects can linger and are often mistaken for personal failure or spiritual weakness. There may be an internalized belief that the individual has failed, without the ability to recognize that it was, in fact, the system that failed them. Instead of acknowledging the harm, many spiritualize their suffering, interpreting it as God testing them or as evidence of unfaithfulness.

In order to cope and survive in such environments, individuals may come to rely on people-pleasing behaviors and self-sacrifice, often to their own detriment. Behaviors that others perceive as being "servant-hearted" may, in reality, reflect a fawning response aimed at avoiding correction, exclusion, or God's disapproval.

This often results in a growing dissonance between the perceived need to maintain spiritual performance and the individual's authentic internal experience. Such dissonance can lead to a persistent sense of being "fake" or a "hypocrite."

Over time, individuals may find it difficult to access anger, sadness, fear, joy, desire, or pleasure. Many have been conditioned to suppress their "negative emotions," including doubt or anxiety. This kind of emotional shutdown is often accompanied by an inner taskmaster pushing for perfection. High levels of self-monitoring of thoughts, emotions, behaviors, or motives may be present. Many were taught to constantly examine themselves for sin.

All of this can culminate in a profound sense of identity confusion. There may be struggles in knowing what is actually believed or wanted, and in making independent decisions and

---

[53] Mate, *The Myth of Normal,* Loc 26, Kindle

choices. Some may often describe themselves as "lost" or "empty" if others cannot tell them what to do or how they should feel or think.

Chronic tension in the body may also result from holding in emotions. Fatigue or burnout, headaches, digestive issues, or chronic pain may result. Some may feel disconnected from their bodies or their intuition. A persistent state of hypervigilance, restlessness, or being on edge may be present. These symptoms are not signs of weakness or lack of faith. They are evidence of a system that demanded too much and gave too little space for humanity. These individuals are not weak—high-control systems are just this powerful.

Trauma can heal through reconnection with your own nervous system and all parts of yourself, and through honest, compassionate relationships with others and with God over time.

Trauma is an injury, and all injuries can heal.

Spiritual Trauma and Shame

During my last break on a typical Friday afternoon at work some time last year, I logged into Facebook to check if anyone had responded to a question I had asked earlier. I was surprised to see the top post from someone I barely knew. It was a picture he had shared, and it had the following message:

Things Jesus never said:
Listen to your heart.
Be true to yourself.
Trust your gut.
Feel good about who you are.
Happiness is what matters.
Just be a good person.

Things Jesus actually said:
If anyone would come after me, let him deny himself
and take up his cross and follow me.
– Matthew 16:24

I felt a bit uneasy for a moment while reading this, then closed all tabs and got ready for my next client. I worked with him to examine some underlying issues, clarify his goals, and develop practical approaches for managing challenges.

After the session, I felt absolutely awful. I sensed a lingering anxiety in me, some tension throughout my whole body, and a mix of uncomfortable emotions I couldn't make sense of. Since I couldn't pinpoint the reason, I closed the door to my office and, before going home from work, asked myself what was going on.

Straight away, I felt a deep sense of shame wash over me. "You have no idea what you're even doing," I heard in my head. "You've devoted your life to something unimportant and ungodly, and you are wrong about what following God even means. None of this matters because you are not denying yourself the right way. You are selfish and self-centered. You need to stop."

Recognizing some shallow breathing taking place, I packed my bag and knowing I needed some fresh air, I went for a walk.

I dragged my feet through one of my favorite parts of the city and could feel my heart racing. Trying to balance staying in the present moment with listening to my painful past learning, I first paid attention to the existence of that Vietnamese restaurant I loved and the languages I heard around me. Next, by listening to myself, I noticed the lump in my throat that had been stopping me from breathing properly and how my anxiety had been growing in intensity.

And I continued to question everything.

Maybe I was really getting this all wrong. Maybe Jesus really meant to deny *everything*—our emotions, our thoughts, our needs, our desires, and our personalities. Maybe he gave them to us only so that we could give them back to him. Deny their existence, push them away. And if we failed, we would miss out on *truly* following him.

As I kept walking, I decided to get on my own side a little bit better. I reminded myself of the things I knew that I knew, based on psychological research, my own lived experience with both faith and trauma, and thousands upon thousands of client stories:

• Denying our needs, wants, emotions, and independent thinking can lead to trauma.
• Denying who we are as individuals can lead to trauma.
• Feeling shamed into compliance can lead to trauma.
• Loving God, myself, and others does not lead to trauma.

I reminded myself that I could also look at how Jesus lived his life in the fullest capacity of compassion, love and understanding, and how he offered hope for the hopeless and strength for the weak in ways the world had never encountered before. I also reminded myself that Isaiah 61:1-2 describes Jesus and his character this way:

The Spirit of the Sovereign Lord is on me, because the Lord has anointed me to proclaim good news to the poor. He has sent me to bind up the brokenhearted, to proclaim freedom for the captives and release from the darkness for the prisoners, to proclaim the year of the Lord's favor and the day of vengeance of our God, to comfort all who mourn.

Then, I reminded myself that it is also written:

The Lord your God is with you, the Mighty Warrior who saves. He will

I reminded myself that shaming others into making black-and-white, either-or choices is a sign of control. I reminded myself that the realities of life often are more complex and nuanced than just one or the other. I reminded myself that, instead of two opposing options, there exists a middle ground that is often unavailable to us in controlling Christian environments.

As I did this, I started breathing deeper, and tears started welling up in me. I had reached the park next to our home, and walking underneath the old fig trees, I let myself cry.

It was pretty hot outside, and I was tired. For a moment, I felt completely defeated by the rigid rules we so often pride ourselves on holding. They may help us feel strong in our faith, immovable in our beliefs, and for sure, better than the rest. They may reinforce a form of Christian discipline that emphasizes inflexible decision-making and finding reassurance in our efforts.

They may also help us overlook mercy, justice, and faithfulness.

This type of shame is too familiar to too many of us. The shame that tells us that if we are not doing it perfectly, we are doing it wrong. The shame that tells us we only have one possible interpretation of the Bible available to us, and if we are not getting it exactly as described, we aren't getting it at all. The shame that yells at us to do more, to deny more, to suppress more, to forget who we are.

It is that type of very special shame that can make us dismiss and forget our real lived experiences, and prevent us from holding complex, nuanced emotions and uncertainties within us. The shame that constantly tells us that we are not good enough, we are not strong enough, we are not trying hard enough, and that we are becoming selfish, rebellious, and too independent.

For me, reading that post took me right back to the time in my life when I was still fighting for the acceptance of those around me. When the only way to survive was to stay stuck in the fawn response, to please and appease, to be all that I was supposed to be so I wouldn't become ostracized, talked about, judged and pitied. Back then, the only correct way to follow God was to push aside all that would naturally arise in me and force myself to agree with the doctrine even when I didn't.

It didn't work very well, and it didn't work very long, but the trauma hit deep. At times, my nervous system still remembers that threat like it happened yesterday.

In high-control groups, these words of Jesus are often weaponized to demand self-suppression—to mute our emotions, override our boundaries, and distrust our inner knowing. It teaches that obedience means silence, and holiness means becoming small enough to never challenge the system.

I believe Jesus' call to deny ourselves presumes an intact, valued self who can freely choose surrender out of love, not fear. It is responsive and relational and can't be reduced to a set of rules or behaviors because God doesn't speak to us in formulas. What he's asking someone to lay down is not necessarily what he's asking of another. Knowing ourselves would mean freedom from comparison and competition, where we can trust that we can hear his guidance in our hearts over the demands around us.

Learning to separate God's voice from the system's voice means becoming attuned to the fruit: the system's voice shames, constricts, and controls; God's voice clarifies, liberates, and restores. True self-denial never erases the self but reveals it.

Genuine self-denial begins with honesty. It allows us to say, "This is what is happening in me," without rushing to fix, hide, or spiritualize it. In that honesty, God can meet the real self, not the persona the system has demanded we become. From here, denying the self can mean letting go of what is untrue and rooted in fear. True transformation grows from truthfulness and encounter, not from shame and compliance.

When we look at how Jesus interacted with people, we see that he often called out hypocrisy, attacked corruption in religious systems, expressed sadness and anger, refused to align with those protecting the system, and constantly disrupted the religious and political status quo. He wasn't always nice to people and made those around him often quite uncomfortable.

For this, he was hated and misunderstood by those in power. Picking up our cross, I believe, is not a call to close our eyes to reality and passively endure abuse, but more of a courage to speak up against legalistic control. I believe it's about choosing solidarity with the oppressed and accepting the cost that will follow when we oppose systemic injustice, just like he did.

We may also be called to deny the false selves we have built to be accepted by the culture around us. We may be called to costly love and personal integrity in faith, where we prioritize truth over image. We may need to start naming the wrongs we see around us and resist the pull to fit in by silencing ourselves. When we do this, we may need to learn how to endure the painful consequences of living according to our real convictions rather than a template offered by a controlling system around us.

This may mean we lose status or relationships for the sake of truth. We may lose the acceptance of the people we have known for years. We may lose our place at the table, our good standing in the community, and the authority our loyalty once gave to us.

Living like this will come with a cost, and reveal who values us for who we are, and who only valued our agreement.

Trauma and Growth in Scripture

"I started believing that I needed constant correction
and guidance just to get through the day."

Trauma is on the pages of the Bible as well. As we read through the many stories about the real people who lived through their real experiences, we can imagine taking on their perspectives and allow ourselves to understand how they might have felt during those times.

Let's take Joseph's story from Genesis 37-50 for our example here, even though we could choose many others. First, we may need to accept that this story is not only about restoration and God's sovereignty. This story is also about betrayal and the long-term consequences of deceit within a dysfunctional family system.

Joseph was 17 when the story began. He was the favored son of Jacob, the firstborn of his favorite wife, Rachel. Jacob gifted him with a special robe, which was a very clear physical marker of preference. Joseph started being bullied by his brothers, as Genesis 37:4 states, "When his brothers saw that their father loved him more than any of them, they hated him and could not speak a kind word to him."

Joseph's brothers seemed to suffer for this. They wanted to be accepted by their dad as Joseph was accepted. Their actions and choices were far from healthy but probably reflected the pain they felt when their parent, who was meant to be fair and love all their kids just the same, showed open favoritism to one of them.

Joseph also had dreams where the interpretation seemed to be that his brothers would one day bow to him. And being a naïve teenager, he shared those dreams with them. This may have been a poor choice at the time, but that is irrelevant to what happened next. What matters is that he was betrayed by his own family.

"Come now, let's kill him and throw him into one of these cisterns and say that a ferocious animal devoured him. Then we'll see what comes of his dreams.' When Reuben heard this, he tried to rescue him from their hands. 'Let's not take his life,' he said. 'Don't shed any blood. Throw him into this cistern here in the wilderness, but don't lay a hand on him.' Reuben said this to rescue him from them and take him back to his father" (Genesis 37:20-22).

As the story continues, we can see that Reuben's plan didn't work. "So when the Midianite merchants came by, his brothers pulled Joseph up out of the cistern and sold him for twenty shekels of silver to the Ishmaelites, who took him to Egypt. When Reuben returned to the cistern and saw that Joseph was not there, he tore his clothes. He went back to his brothers and said, 'The boy isn't there! Where can I turn now?' Then they got Joseph's robe, slaughtered a goat and dipped the robe in the blood. They took the ornate robe back to their father and said, 'We found this. Examine it to see whether it is your son's robe'" (Genesis 37:28-32).

First, Joseph's brothers planned to kill him, then threw him into a pit, and then sold him to slave traders passing by. After this, his brothers staged his death. They brought the news of Joseph's death back to their father, who, of course, was absolutely devastated by the news.

Grieving for the loss of a child can take a whole lifetime in different ways. This was Jacob's trauma. Joseph's brothers also lied to their father in his mourning. They lied to the whole community. They knew the truth of what had happened but said nothing to right their wrongs. They watched their own parent crumble to pieces due to the loss of their son. They even tried to comfort him in his grief, which compounds the betrayal (Genesis 37:35). The truth stayed hidden for years. This is emotionally abusive behavior and deception. Those who not only harmed their own brother but also let their father suffer under these false assumptions.

The Bible doesn't describe how Joseph felt as he was taken into slavery. But any realistic understanding of trauma tells us that he must have experienced despair, and terror—any one of us would have. Joseph was stripped of his identity, violently and abruptly forced out of his family and larger community and relocated to a foreign country with no support system, at 17 years old.

Joseph's real comfort was God's presence in his life: "Now Joseph had been taken down to Egypt. Potiphar, an Egyptian who was one of Pharaoh's officials, the captain of the guard, bought him from the Ishmaelites who had taken him there. The LORD was with Joseph so that he prospered, and he lived in the house of his Egyptian master. When his master saw that the LORD was with him and that the LORD gave him success in everything he did, Joseph found favor in his eyes and became his attendant. Potiphar put him in charge of his household, and entrusted to his care everything he owned" (Genesis 39:1-4).

Now, it would make things a bit too simple if we believed that Joseph didn't continue to have real, human emotions during this time. He was still a young boy who was away from his family after being mistreated by his brothers. He must have known that his parents back home now thought he was dead. Pain and God's favor don't cancel each other out.

Later in the story, Joseph was falsely accused of sexual assault by Potiphar's wife and imprisoned for it. Again, Scripture doesn't explain his internal battles here, but we can imagine how he must have felt in another unjust situation he had to face. He had to go through many traumatic events in his lifetime.

"But while Joseph was there in the prison, the LORD was with him; he showed him kindness and granted him favor in the eyes of the warden" (Genesis 39:20-21). I am certain that God being so near him through all this was one of the key reasons why he was able to stay resilient in his suffering and wait to be freed from captivity. The relationship he had with God was his very real anchor during his very real trauma.

Joseph grew in wisdom, but we don't know about the personal struggles he must have had during these years. How he must have missed home and his family. How out of place he must have felt. How he must have endured feeling alone, forgotten, and mistreated. All of these emotions, and many more, would have been the most natural, human reactions to what he had to go through. We know he wanted to get out of the prison when he explained to one of the other prisoners, the cupbearer, "But when all goes well with you, remember me and show me kindness; mention me to Pharaoh and get me out of this prison. I was forcibly carried off from the land of the Hebrews, and even here I have done nothing to deserve being put in a dungeon" (Genesis 40:14-15). Joseph was not oblivious to the truth and injustice of his story—and he remained in prison for two more years after this.

We know he was eventually freed to explain the Pharaoh's dreams, which he did correctly: "Seven years of great abundance are coming throughout the land of Egypt, but seven years of famine will follow them. Then all the abundance in Egypt will be forgotten, and the famine will ravage the land" (Genesis 41:29-30). Very quickly after this, he was put in charge of the whole land of Egypt at the age of 30. Even though this was a real miracle and Joseph ended up saving many lives during the famine, he was still out of place. Egypt was not his home. He was a migrant who had lived years of his life with very limited social circles, without any friends of his age. And yet, he was able to recognize God's hand on his life, "Joseph named his firstborn Manasseh and said, 'It is because God has made me forget all my trouble and all my father's household.' The second son he named Ephraim and said, 'It is because God has made me fruitful in the land of my suffering'" (Genesis 41:51-52).

Meanwhile, his brothers kept living with their secret. By doing this, they kept emotionally manipulating their own father and the whole community around them while maintaining the appearance of being supportive sons.

When Joseph had risen to power in Egypt, his brothers arrived during the famine seeking food and help. "Then ten of Joseph's brothers went down to buy grain from Egypt. But Jacob did not send Benjamin, Joseph's brother, with the others, because he was afraid that harm might come to him" (Genesis 42:3-4). As we have learned, trauma imprints experiences of threat in our nervous systems, so even long after the event, our bodies may respond to reminders of that threat as if danger is happening again. To me, it sounds like Jacob was experiencing a very understandable trauma response in this part of the story.

"Now Joseph was the governor of the land, the person who sold grain to all its people. So when Joseph's brothers arrived, they bowed down to him with their faces to the ground" (Genesis 42:6). They didn't recognize Joseph, but he recognized them. Joseph didn't immediately reveal who he was, but instead, he kept testing them for honesty and transformation. This reveals the hurt he had been through and the mistrust he had been carrying for years. We can't rush to the point of the story where we only see restoration and forgiveness, but we can see that Joseph was not ready to reconcile with his brothers straight away. First, he observed them, evaluated them, and *withheld trust until he saw evidence of change.*

This is a healthy response and a good set of boundaries to hold when we have been betrayed by others. When trust has been broken, it cannot be restored by an apology alone, especially if the harm has gone unacknowledged for years. This was a test of character, and Joseph needed to see if his brothers carried a new understanding and remorse for their actions.

Joseph only revealed who he was, weeping loudly, once he saw one of his brothers show genuine concern for their father's well-being after he volunteered to stay in Egypt as a slave in place of their youngest brother Benjamin. This is the first time in the story that Joseph can see compassion and responsibility from any of the brothers. We don't, of course, know the guilt and regret many or all of them had possibly lived with for all these years, working hard to cover up the betrayal they had fabricated years prior.

Joseph showed incredible kindness to them that can only come through genuine, transformative healing. He saw God's hand in everything that had happened to him and was convinced of his goodness. This does not erase the suffering he had endured when he was younger. Trauma and the goodness of God can coexist, and often do, in our lives.

When the brothers returned to their home in Canaan and told Jacob, their dad, that Joseph was still alive, we can only imagine what went through Jacob's mind. He learned that his other sons knew the truth all along. We don't know how Jacob reacted to finding out this horrific betrayal, but we can imagine. For years, his own sons had manipulated him into a false reality. He had grieved and suffered while trusting his own family, who deceived him in a disturbingly cruel way.

This is often what happens in trauma: we don't only experience loss but have to face the realization that the people we trusted were the ones enabling or perpetuating the harm. The comfort we can see here is that the truth tends to eventually come out, and people are freed from the burden of their own lies.

The story ends with Joseph telling his brothers, "You intended to harm me, but God intended it for good to accomplish what is now being done, the saving of many lives" (Genesis 50:20). This shows Joseph's personal experience of God's faithfulness in the midst of all the hardships. It does not explain away pain or erase the suffering he had endured.

Such a positive perspective can be explained as *post-*

traumatic growth. This is the stage in healing and recovery where those who have endured psychological distress can often see positive changes in themselves, their character, and their outlook on life afterward. In this stage, people no longer need to feel through the anguish and anxiety as deeply or as often, but are ready to genuinely move forward with a deeper understanding of themselves, God, others, and the painful situations they have had to move through. Post-traumatic growth often shows up as new appreciation for life, healthier relationships with others, seeing new possibilities in life, recognizing personal strengths, and deeper, more personal faith.

Joseph showed these signs in the way he responded to his brothers, which is why I think he had worked through his trauma well and not skipped over it, because it takes intentionality to get to this point in recovery. Growth can't be forced or manufactured. but can flow freely when healing is experienced authentically.

After walking through the valleys of pain, many can later see that they've grown in resilience. They know how to better set boundaries with others. And they often want to help others and raise awareness in the areas where people still need to see change.

Post-traumatic growth doesn't say that the painful experiences were always necessary. Rather, it accepts the pain but welcomes recovery. Growth is the diamond in the rough and a knowing that God is able to use anything for his purposes.

What Trauma Is Not

> "I was told to give it all to God.
> How do you even do that?"

To understand trauma even better, it may help if we clarify what it is not, so that we can tell the difference between healing and the pressure to appear healed. Knowing what happens in many of our churches can hopefully help us see human suffering through a more compassionate lens.

- **Trauma is not weakness.** Having a trauma response means the nervous system is reacting normally to something it recognizes as overwhelming or threatening. It *does not* mean people are being dramatic, don't understand or can't access God's peace, or don't believe enough.

- **Trauma is not a lack of faith, a "spirit of accusation," or spiritual immaturity.** Trauma is the body's perfectly human response to harm. It *does not* signal weak faith, unbelief, rebellion, or sin.

- **Trauma is not an offense.** Trauma arises from harm that overwhelms the nervous system. It *is not* the same as just being upset.

- **Trauma is not unforgiveness.** Trauma responses are the brain and the body's way of coping with harm. Forgiveness, when chosen, *does not* erase the physiological response the nervous system holds when trauma remains unresolved.

- **Trauma is not something people can simply "pray away" or "give to God."** Trauma leaves its imprint on the nervous system and brain. It *can't be* erased by spiritual disciplines alone.

- **Trauma is not just feeling upset or stressed.** Trauma is a physiological response to harm. It *is not* every disagreement, heated argument, or season of stress.

- **Trauma is not a choice.** Trauma is an involuntary survival response to something the brain detects as overwhelming and sees as a threat to a person's safety and agency. It *is not* a decision to be weak or unfaithful.

- **Trauma is not permanent brokenness.** Trauma is an injury. Trauma *does not* define people's identity. It also *does not* say anything about their faith or character, but it may say quite a lot about the environments they have been in and the experiences they have lived through.

Chapter Twelve
The Impact of Religious Trauma

"How long, LORD? Will you forget me forever? How long will you hide your face from me? How long must I wrestle with my thoughts and day after day have sorrow in my heart?"
— Psalm 13:1-2

"I don't know how to make decisions on my own."

Having named the reality of religious trauma, we will now focus on learning more about its impact on our well-being. There are some common ways this harm is often experienced by those recovering from control and abuse. Instead of just abstract symptoms, there are real, lived consequences for many who have been bruised in such environments. These can all be resolved through healing and time but are often felt as the painful reality for those recovering from this type of harm.

Sarah Perry, in her article *Religious/Spiritual Abuse, Meaning-Making, and Posttraumatic Growth* writes about these challenges this way:

"The aftermath of Religious/Spiritual abuse can have profound and far-reaching effects, permeating various aspects of an individual's well-being, including psychological, emotional, and spiritual dimensions."[54]

---

[54] Perry, Sarah. "Religious/Spiritual Abuse, Meaning-Making, and Posttraumatic Growth." *Religions* 15, no. 7 (2024): 824.

These include, but are not limited to:

- Symptoms akin to post-traumatic stress disorder
- Depression, anxiety, and self-harm tendencies
- Profound spiritual insecurity
- Grief, shame, and existential disorientation
- Maladaptive coping mechanisms such as eating disorders or addictions, or engaging in dysfunctional relationships
- Ruptures with faith, anger towards God
- Retraumatization in the faith community through stigmatization, isolation, shaming, and hostility
- Retraumatization after sharing about one's trauma through victim-blaming, denial, disbelief, and abandonment by the faith community

The effects of religious trauma reach far beyond the moments of harm because it touches people's capacity to trust and feel safe, no matter how much they love God. Trauma's impact is also not measured by comparison, but by how deeply it affects people's sense of safety and trust. It exists on a sliding scale, and if you now find yourself unsure where you sit on that scale, reach out for professional support. Needing recovery for the mind should be as natural and accepted as seeing a doctor when your bones are broken. Our minds deserve tending and correct, skilled care just the same.

Healing is available to everyone and not reserved for a few. Even the most fragile parts of us can be restored, slowly, in relationships that are safe.

Moral Injury

"I feel ashamed of myself when I look back
on the things I taught to others."

While trauma often wounds us through loss of safety and agency, moral injury strikes differently—it pierces our sense of right and wrong. Moral injury refers to the internal suffering that occurs when people are forced to act in ways that go against their own moral compass or ethical beliefs and values. While the term originally gained attention in military and healthcare contexts, it is increasingly recognized as originating in high-control environments, where personal agency is often suppressed.

In these settings, moral injury is usually reinforced by a theology that equates unquestioned submission with righteousness and discourages any pushback in the name of faith. People in these communities are usually trained to distrust their internal responses and to override feelings of discomfort or distress with religious justification. Over time, this can lead to a fractured sense of self, where their moral instincts are dulled or overridden, and their identities become entangled with the role they are expected to play in the system.

Three common types of moral injury are:

• **Act of Commission.** People may carry moral injury from moments when they actively participated in something that violated their core values. This could include enforcing rules, delivering messages, or making decisions that caused others harm, even if they believed it was the right or necessary thing to do at the time. Looking back, many may feel conflicted, ashamed, or unsure how to reconcile what they did to others with who they believe themselves to be.

• **Act of Omission.** People may also carry moral injury from what they didn't do. These are the times when they witnessed harm but didn't speak up, didn't intervene, or stayed silent in order to avoid punishment or loss. They may have felt that taking action would have risked too much. Later, the sense that they failed to protect others and their families can become a source of regret or self-blame.

• **Betrayal.** This form of moral injury can happen when someone in authority, especially someone people trusted, directs them to act in ways that conflict with their sense of right and wrong. They may have followed their leaders out of obedience, loyalty, or fear. Over time, they may come to realize that the very people or systems they looked to for spiritual guidance caused them to violate their own moral boundaries. Betrayal like this can affect their ability to trust others and themselves.

Moral injury is a common impact, especially in those who were deeply committed to their faith and their community. Contrary to these communities' beliefs, people now injured by the culture were usually not the ones who always lacked faith and character, but who yearned to learn more, and worked really hard to shape their whole lives around the teachings of their faith community. They often did everything they could to please leaders, stay loyal to the system with sincerity, and align their inner world with external expectations. When things didn't feel right, they assumed the problem was within themselves. Rather than questioning the structure, they questioned their own faith or worthiness.

When these people are faced with inconsistencies and harm within their communities, they often spend months or even years trying to find fault within themselves, believing there is something wrong with them for not feeling okay about everything they are now seeing. The last thing they want to do is to dismantle their belief system and be left to repair what's been broken. More often than not, I've seen these individuals come to therapy desperately trying to stay in their faith communities, not to leave them.

Therefore, it is usually the more faithful, loyal and committed ones who are most impacted by moral injury. They are often people who didn't realize they were behaving contrary to their own values, because they had never had the chance to explore their own morals and values prior to behaving in the expected ways.

These are some of the injuries people often recognize:

- **Staying silent during public shaming.** People may have witnessed someone being publicly corrected, humiliated, or labeled as sinful. Even though it made them uncomfortable in the moment, they didn't defend them, either because they didn't feel safe enough to do so or because they believed at the time it was "biblical discipline." Later, they may regret their silence.
- **Participating in the shunning of a member.** People may have been instructed to cut off communication with someone who left the group or was labeled as rebellious. They might have obeyed out of fear of spiritual consequences or social rejection, but now struggle with regret about abandoning that relationship.
- **Teaching or promoting harmful doctrine.** People may have led a Bible study, preached a sermon, or counseled someone using teachings they now see as damaging. At the time, they believed they were doing the right thing but now carry the weight of what those words may have done to others.

- **Forcing others, or themselves, into exhausting service**. People may have pushed themselves or others to serve out of obligation, without any boundaries. They may have ignored all the signs of burnout or illness because they were told that sacrifice was the highest form of spiritual maturity. Later, they may realize how that service crossed widely understood ethical, legal, or personal boundaries.

- **Policing others' behavior and reporting them to leadership**. People may have been encouraged to monitor other members' "spiritual health" and report any signs of sin or doubt to the leadership team. Participating in this kind of surveillance may have made them feel uncomfortable, but they were told it was necessary to protect the purity of the group.

- **Looking away from abuse or manipulation by leadership**. People may have seen or heard things that didn't sit well with them, like emotional control, exploitation, or spiritual bypassing and abuse, but justified it all as "strong leadership" or assumed the victim must be exaggerating. Now, the realization that they didn't do anything about this sooner may feel like a betrayal of their own values.

- **Choosing not to leave for the sake of belonging**. People may have stayed in the system long after their conscience started raising alarms. They may have prioritized community, family, or a sense of spiritual safety over their own values. That choice, even if very understandable, may now feel like a hurtful moral compromise.

Healing from moral injury takes time but can start by accepting the truth about one's whole experience. This can look like naming the moments when individuals betrayed their own values and recognizing the seasons when they conformed in order to survive. When this work is undertaken, it is important to remain mindful not to fall into self-condemnation, but rather to acknowledge the impossible bind that was imposed. A great deal of compassion is needed for the version of the self who was trying to make it all work in an environment that punished authenticity and autonomy but framed it as faithfulness to God.

When individuals reconnect with their internal sense of right and wrong, it is common to experience grief, anger, or fear. These are all signs of a separation from the version of the self they thought they had to be to measure up, and a movement toward becoming the person they were originally created to be.

Restoring a sense of moral integrity also involves reclaiming agency. It may require setting boundaries with people or institutions that continue to demand silence or compliance. Some may choose to speak out about past harms to realign with core values. Healing comes through integrating all aspects of one's story and all parts of the self in a compassionate, accepting way, over time.

When Trauma Robs All Trust and Faith

"I stopped sensing God's presence entirely."

There are moments when life can feel like it has stripped away every reason to believe. When the prayers that once carried hope now echo back in silence. When faith starts to feel like the very thing that hurts. It's in these places that some no longer know how to trust God after everything that's happened.

Maybe this is you.

Maybe you've faced such a shattering of faith that nothing you've been taught about God feels compatible with what actually happened to you. Maybe you've had to face one trauma after another, each one layering over the last until it all blurs together. You've prayed, pleaded, and followed faithfully. You've said yes over and over, only to find yourself broken by the sins of others.

And suddenly you have been left with one of the most difficult questions you've ever had to ask: *How can a good Father watch his child suffer like this and not intervene?*

What you've had to live through feels cruel. It feels unreasonable. It feels like abandonment. It feels like the opposite of love. This is a true, emotionally accurate response to pain, and anyone who tries to explain it away hasn't lived through what you did. Because when the pain is real, you don't want a theory of God. You want a God who would have stopped it.

And he didn't.

I don't think there's any tidy way to reconcile a Father's goodness with his silence during your suffering. There just isn't. You can't spiritualize the moment you needed to be rescued and weren't.

What you can do is tell the truth.

Trauma can deeply affect the way you view God. It can become a lens through which you see yourself and the foundation you used to stand on. After trauma, faith can no longer be black and white. It can't be filled with certainties, easy answers, or go-to Scriptures you say without thinking them through. Trauma changes all that.

If faith collapses after trauma, it isn't a spiritual failure. It's a physiological response. If your nervous system has learned to brace for danger, it cannot easily surrender to trust, not even to God. Maybe your soul stopped believing because your body has been on high alert for too long.

Your body remembers what hurt and it protects you the only way it knows how. Healing begins when you stop shaming those protections and start listening to them.

Your body always speaks the truth. It speaks the truth

about the experiences you've lived through, the relationships in your life, and all the moments when you pushed through your body's cues for danger.

When my nervous system was dysregulated after reading the post, the danger wasn't in that moment. There was nothing dangerous about the post. My body, however, recognized the dualistic tone and interpreted it as loss of connection, failure, and gatekeeping. This is all true and happened to me. That's why my body shifted into a threat response and told me to run away or hide—it recognized all the painful past learning it had survived years prior.

Healing is the steady unlearning of danger. It's letting the body discover that it no longer has to stand guard. And as the body softens, the soul often finds room to return to what it lost. This doesn't usually happen in a sudden revelation but gradually, over time.

And when trust starts to build, faith can follow.

Chapter Thirteen

Bruised by Belief

*"The LORD is close to the brokenhearted
and saves those who are crushed in spirit."*
— Psalm 34:18

"I thought the world made sense
but now I can see I had things lined up all wrong.
What now?"

Throughout this book, we have explored some red flags of control and how control can impact our psychological and spiritual health. I know it's been a lot to take in. Before we discuss healing more, here are some conclusions we have drawn so far:

In high-control Christian groups, there is no real freedom to **think independently**. If we choose to express our questions, there is typically no space for discussion, only correction or punishment, which are viewed as forms of discipleship. Over time, we often come to believe that our independent thoughts are wrong and the group's teachings are right.

Prohibiting independent thought can lead to **enmeshed relationships**, where we may begin to believe that submission and obedience to leadership are the only important aspects of our Christian walk, overlooking everything else.

Living in a controlling Christian environment can significantly hurt our **sense of self.** We may struggle to trust that our bodies, emotions, and thoughts accurately reflect how we are doing, and instead, we learn to rely on others to tell us how we should be feeling. As a result, we may lack a strong sense of identity.

In a high-control environment, we also struggle with

establishing **healthy boundaries.** This can manifest as chronic oversharing and excessive repentance, saying yes to everything asked of us, worrying about how others perceive us, and working hard to gain the approval of our group.

We may also lack **emotional freedom.** Just as there are consequences for thinking freely, there are consequences for feeling and expressing emotions in high-control systems. From others' reactions, we may mistakenly conclude that some emotions are more spiritual than others, which is simply not true. This belief can prevent us from knowing and accepting ourselves and others unconditionally.

All of this can impact our **discernment.** We may come to see everything that naturally arises within us as a sign of rebellion and sin, and we might start disregarding God's voice within us that contradicts the rigid template we have been given.

In an environment like this, our faith in Christ and spiritual disciplines may not be able to flow as a source of freedom and life within us; instead, they become a set of behaviors we feel obligated to maintain without question. All the life-giving practices, such as prayer and meditating on God's Word, can turn into ways to avoid honest observation, authentic feeling, and speaking up when needed.

All of this can foster a culture that **prioritizes the system and its leaders over the individuals** who are hurting, leading to an inability or unwillingness to observe our surroundings honestly and accurately. In such a culture of silence, many can end up **bruised and traumatized** by control.

In this section, we have named these wounds correctly, as we need to learn how to speak the truth about this issue. I want to invite you to refuse to minimize the depth of trauma's impact on others, or on yourself. This is not the end of our story, though. Even though we now know that unhealthy systems can leave people wounded, we can also trust that safe systems can help us heal.

In the next section, we will turn the corner from recognizing the harm to healing and building healthy faith communities together. These communities are marked by honesty, freedom, compassion, and safety. They are communities where we are welcomed to belong, not just fit in.

Part Four
Rebuilding

Chapter Fourteen
Inner and Relational Healing

*"Carry each other's burdens, and in this way
you will fulfill the law of Christ."*
– Galatians 6:2

"I've finally been able to make sense of it all."

God created our brain, and he created our nervous system's stress response. He knows all about fight, flight, fawn, and freeze. He's the author and maker of our whole system: our cognition, emotions, subconscious processes, and attachment. He knows our trauma responses are physiological, not a lack of anything. He knows that trauma leads to fragmentation, where the individuals impacted by traumatic events start to live in disconnection from their bodies, sometimes leading to disconnection from him. They may still want to find God but feel totally unable to do so due to their wounding.

God is well aware of trauma, and I believe that we should be too.

Healing leads to wholeness. It leads to integrating all the parts of the self and the painful stories that may have been suppressed before. And through this healing, the wounded can start to find God again as someone who never left, even though it may have felt like he did.

For those who have experienced religious trauma, healing begins with reestablishing emotional and physiological safety. When one's attachment to God, community, or spiritual authority has long been intertwined with fear or harm, the nervous system may learn that faith itself is unsafe. What will be essential for recovery is safety: finding environments, relationships, and inner practices that signal to the body, mind, and soul that you are no longer in danger.

Often, those who have experienced trauma feel unsafe both externally (in their environment) and internally (within themselves). This, from what I have observed, can delay recovery for those coming from high-control faith cultures; as people in these systems are not safely allowed to challenge their leaders' decisions, teachings or the group's doctrine and overall culture, and honestly view them as harmful even when they are, they don't recognize feeling unsafe in their environments, only within themselves. As adequate trauma knowledge is not usually available in these cultures, trauma is often mistakenly believed to be a lack of character, spiritual disciplines and faith.

Trauma is not a choice between fear and faith. It is not a battle of right and wrong. It's not healed through service, discipline, or self-sacrifice. As we've discussed before, trauma is an involuntary response and won't be healed by force, but in safety and connection, over time. Trauma will start to heal when the body starts to feel safe again.

Dr. Beth Argot says that traumatized people don't hear what we have to say to them in church before they have had the opportunity to heal from their trauma. Our messages, no matter how good, won't land well before the trauma has been seen, the person heard, and safety established. This is why trauma healing needs to matter to our groups of faith.[55] After trauma, safety needs to be established by helping the nervous system settle. People need space to notice and recognize the state of their body, slow down, and be seen and heard without judgment. This can look like taking a few slow, deep breaths, feeling the feet on the ground, or gently stretching to release tension.

Psychiatrist and trauma researcher Judith Herman introduced a central framework in trauma therapy, the three-stage recovery model, which will help us understand the process of healing. We will look at how these stages can be used in our churches as well. The three stages of healing are **Safety and Stabilization**, **Remembrance and Mourning**, and **Reconnection and Reintegration**.[56] Here are some ways we can make sure we build communities that don't harm but help people recover:

Safety and Stabilization – trust anchors, hope grows. In this stage of trauma recovery, people injured by harm are working to feel physiologically, emotionally, and spiritually safe. They may have been through relational and systemic betrayal and now experience deep layers of mistrust. In church, this might look like them avoiding leadership structures, small groups, prayer ministry, or any advice. They may sometimes appear skeptical, distant, and angry at spiritual (often loaded) language. They may set boundaries very close to themselves and prefer to observe quietly rather than participate.

They may share how God feels distant or absent in their lives. They may say that he doesn't speak anymore. You may see them seeking God through nature, art, or meditation rather than church worship. Many of us may have heard that the biggest

---

55 Beth Argot, "When the Brain Can't Hear God - Understanding Trauma and Disconnection," Dallas Theological Seminary 2025
56 "Three-Stage Recovery Model," *Counselling Tutor*, counsellingtutor.com

hurdle for us in hearing God's voice is a lack of faith. I don't believe this to be true. I believe it's unresolved trauma.

The way we respond to people in this stage of healing can impact their process profoundly. Here are some ways you can help:

- Respect autonomy – don't pressure them to join, trust you, or forgive those who hurt them.
- Acknowledge power dynamics – emphasize choice, consent, and transparency in all church activities.
- Model safety – consistency, honesty, and gentle boundaries build trust more than words do.
- Avoid spiritual bypassing – don't use faith language to rush or reframe their pain. They are not "hard-hearted" when they don't hear you; they are signaling that trust hasn't yet been proven and built.

Remembrance and Mourning – share the story, bear witness, and grieve. This is the next stage of healing, where people start to gradually share their story. It is a good sign as it can show that trust has been established more, both internally and externally. They may begin to process what happened to them, often with waves of anger, sadness, and confusion. They may revisit painful memories of control, exclusion, isolation, or them fawning for years of their lives. They might begin to question doctrines more vocally and express their grief more openly. They may show intense emotions and struggle to know how to feel towards their faith.

We may see people reconnecting with God through Scripture, learning, and studying. This is the stage of truth-telling and integration, where the fragmented parts of themselves and their stories can become whole again.

This is how you can help:

- Listen without defending the institution – avoid the urge to explain, justify, or minimize their experiences.
- Validate their pain before offering perspectives – say "That must have been terrifying" instead of "There are no perfect churches." Churches don't need to be perfect; they just need to not control and abuse.
- Hold space for lament – the whole community can incorporate practice of communal lament, storytelling, and art that honors grief.
- Protect confidentiality and agency – other people's stories are not yours to share.

Reconnection and Integration – from surviving to living in wholeness. This is where trust and autonomy keep growing. People impacted by trauma keep learning how to reconnect with safe people and reimagining faith that feels authentic and real. They no longer want to have anything to do with controlling systems but instead form something new. In church, we might see them using their voice and gifts again, but with discernment and boundaries. They may develop a more nuanced, personal faith that steps away from hurting people with certainty. They want, and often ask for, mutuality, equality, and truth in all their relationships.

In their relationship with God, we may see them returning to prayer and worship from a place of choice. They may start to have experiences of God as safe and loving again, instead of controlling or punitive. We may see them move towards helping others who are navigating through religious and spiritual trauma.

This is how you can respond:

- Empower participation without control – offer opportunities for contribution that leave space for personal agency.
- Celebrate questions and differences – life is often complex, and we can honor that.
- Affirm identity – see the person not as "broken and restored" but as wise, resilient, and whole.

This is how true healing can start. Sarah Perry, in her article *Religious/Spiritual Abuse, Meaning-Making, and Posttraumatic Growth* says, "Without recognition that abuse was experienced, integrating any traumatic experiences into one's life narrative becomes challenging."[57] Recognizing abuse as abuse and control as control are the keys that open the door for healing.

She also adds that healing comes through sharing our story and being validated in our experience. Controlling environments are not safe to share our story in, unless they check their practices and ways they collectively listen to those who have been hurt.

In this final section, we will discuss healing and then look at ways to discern when it may be time to boldly walk away from a high-control environment, what to expect while you recover and then how to make sure we build healthy faith communities that don't inflict harm in the future. Please note that this book is not intended to replace personal therapy in any way. If you have noticed some bruising inside of you, I highly recommend reaching out for professional help.

There is power in telling your story. When you share what you have lived through with people who will listen and believe you, you can start making sense of all those confusing moments.

Before you can start sharing your story with others, I invite

---

57 Perry, Sarah. "Religious/Spiritual Abuse, Meaning-Making, and Posttraumatic Growth," *Religions* 15, no. 7 (2024): 824.

you to turn towards all the parts of yourself that may have stayed silent before. You are invited to turn towards the hurting and hidden parts of yourself and learn to see these parts as valuable. You may also turn towards the narratives you have been forcing yourself to believe, even in moments you didn't. You did that to survive, so of course, you said yes to them. You can turn toward the very core of yourself that can't ever be taken from you, the inmost being created in his image and cherished in each of us (Psalm 139:13).

You can also gently turn toward your Inner Critic, who has been working hard to keep you safe from others' disapproval. You can turn towards the vulnerable parts of yourself who have been trying hard to measure up to the expectations around you. The parts that have stayed unseen and exhausted.

You are also invited to turn towards others who have suffered. You can turn towards their stories without judgment and listen to their experiences with compassion. And you are invited just to stay there, not to fix them, not to give advice, not even to know and understand everything. You can just be with them.

I also want to invite you to consider what we've discussed so far in possibly a new way. Reflect on the stories of control and religious trauma you've read about or have perhaps experienced yourself. I believe all of us have a question to answer: *How do I want to respond to people's stories from now on?* If this topic matters to you, maybe it's time to stop being silent about it. Many people around you are still suffering quietly, unsure where they can go to be heard and remain safe.

I want to make sure I say this as clearly as I can: if you choose to share your story with me, I will not spiritually bypass you, or offer quick advice or "disciple" you, as it would be inappropriate in this context. I will not try to control you emotionally. I won't victim-blame you or downplay what you went through. I commit to being a safe person to share with.

Chapter Fifteen

When Healing Requires Walking Away

"It is for freedom that Christ has set us free. Stand firm, then,
and do not let yourselves be burdened again by a yoke of slavery."
– Galatians 5:1

"I can't stay knowing all this."

A few years back, I had this dream: I was standing at the foot of what looked like a towering grey mountain. With me were just a few others, watching as a great number of people were drawn toward this mountain-like formation, attached to the strings of a puppeteer. All these people were sucked into these religious systems and turned into marionettes, moving only in formation as the puppeteer allowed.

The masses on this marionette mountain were staggering. The few of us, standing on our own two feet, looking in, felt quite small in front of the mountain of different organizations, denominations, and churches, all run by one puppeteer: control.

Many more people began cutting off their strings. After they got untangled and freed from the mountain of marionettes, they looked as if all their strength was gone, sitting down with their lifeless arms and legs, beaten down by the weight of the control they had lived under.

They looked like survivors who had just washed ashore after a shipwreck, trying to catch their breath. Over time, little by little, these wounded, bruised, and tired marionettes began healing from their injuries, becoming stronger individuals who began to stand firm.

For some, healing can take place within a faith community when there is room for honesty and repair. But for others, the wounds keep cutting too deep if the system proves itself unwilling to change. In such cases, the hope of healing from within gives way to the painful reality that staying only prolongs the harm. Leaving will be necessary for some of you because safety and spiritual health cannot always coexist with loyalty to a destructive system.

Discerning When It's Time to Leave

I understand if leaving your faith community was the last thing you wanted to even consider doing. Realizing its practices as controlling and seeing control as abuse may feel like the ultimate betrayal of everything you believed you were serving. I also understand that it's not all bad; it never has been. But by calling things by their actual names, we may not be able to dismiss this problem any longer.

I know this is a serious, very personal step to take for many. I understand if this feels difficult. The process of leaving (or bringing change) often starts with cracks on the surface. These points may help you see if the process of leaving has already started for you, even if you're still within your community. The more of these fit, the more you may have started seeing the truth about harm:

• You have started to notice gaps between what's preached and what's practiced.
• You can no longer ignore or tolerate hypocrisy or harm, even when others around you seem to be able to close their eyes to it.
• You have felt drawn to ask "Why?" or "Is this really right or necessary?"

• You have felt restless or even hopeless when nothing is changing or when people say, "It's always been this way, and this is God's way."

• You know you are motivated by care, not ego, when you have brought up these issues in conversation. Even so, you may have been told you are rebellious, difficult, or rock the boat for no reason, or you may not be fully welcomed and included as you are.

• You have started feeling heavy grief and burden for people being hurt or excluded by the system.

• You have tried having honest conversations about the need for change within the community, but have often hit walls, silence, excuses, spiritual gaslighting or accusations.

• You may have started feeling more comfortable in the grey areas of thinking than in black-and-white rules.

• You have started to wonder if you are the only one who sees what you now see.

Noticing these cracks on the surface is often the door we need to open before we are ready to pay closer attention to what is happening inside us. From here, you are also invited to listen to these inner signals:

- Do you experience persistent exhaustion? Do you feel drained, anxious, or heavy after gatherings or other interactions with your faith community?

- Have you experienced loss of self-trust? Do you often find yourself doubting your own perceptions or conscience? Do you believe all your discomfort is your own doing and fault?

- Do you silence yourself? Do you keep quiet because you don't want to be judged by others?

- Are you familiar with chronic guilt or fear? What would change in your behavior if you stopped making decisions under pressure or when you feel you must?

- Have you noticed feeling disconnected from yourself? Do you hide parts of who you are from yourself, God, and others?
- Do you experience inner dissonance? Are you familiar with the tension that comes from believing that everything about you is bad when it goes against your faith community's teachings?
- Do you secretly long for freedom?

These cues are your heart's way of drawing attention to what your mind may have tried to explain away. Ignoring them may keep you in familiar surroundings moving forward as well, but it also risks deepening the harm. Listening to your inner world with curiosity can create space for discernment: asking whether your current community can support you in healing or whether healing needs to happen outside its walls.

"There were things, for sure," Emily responded when I asked if she had ever felt that God was leading her to leave the controlling faith environment she was in. She explained a culture with both positive and negative aspects, one that had helped her grow in many ways, yet also burdened her with control. On one hand, their group had done a lot for the city they lived in, but on the other, they were also surrounded by such heavy, loaded language that it had started changing their understanding of reality.

Emily shared about a time when she had begun feeling increasingly anxious and uneasy but kept suppressing her experiences. She was unsure if she should stay in full-time ministry or make her exit, and she kept begging God for a clear yes or no, something she could follow without question, but she did not receive that answer.

During this time, her leader took the opportunity to teach the whole group about situations like these. He said, "If you don't know what to do, trust that God has given your leaders wisdom for you."

If it is not clear by now, this is a major red flag of control. Bottom line is and must be that you are the expert of your own life, living in connection with God, and no one should ever believe they have been given more wisdom about your life than you have for yourself. In moments and seasons of our confusion and questions, wrestling with it all can be incredibly challenging. It will be crucial for you to find people around you who are willing to support you in your wrestling, hold your hands up when you have no strength, and give you wise counsel instead of telling you what to do.

However, Emily believed the teaching she received and overstayed her commitment because her leader felt it was the only right option for her moving forward. The problem was not ill will; it was a lack of boundaries and understanding of personal domain. "Now, looking back, I clearly remember never having peace about staying longer. I was tired, felt unheard, had panic attacks, and experienced increasing levels of anxiety and pain. I had no language for the unrest inside me, so I had no reason to trust my real experience in my own life. The whole system had taught me never to trust my gut, but always to trust my leaders, even when they were wrong. Maybe this was the first time God was teaching me to trust myself over blindly doing what I was told, but I didn't take it. I am learning it now."

During therapy, Emily learned to recognize control and its impacts on her. She learned to trust her inner experiences better and believe that what happened to her had actually happened to her. She is doing much better now, outside of this system of control, which wasn't open to change at the time.

A faith community that is unwilling to change may keep causing more harm and keep retraumatizing the traumatized. This is why it is important to know that leaving may be the only healthy option available to some of you moving forward. Communities that take these questions seriously, repent from causing harm and promise (openly, vocally) to build healthier structures may become places of healing in the future.

Here's how you can practice discerning if your faith community is *not* changing:

- **The same issues persist, no matter how often or in what way you raise them.** Maybe you have tried speaking respectfully, and you have done it often. Maybe you have tried working with the leadership team, not against it. Maybe you have prayed and pleaded, and all you see are some surface-level changes that still protect the deeper layers of the issue.

- **You are punished for honest conversations, and you notice people around you self-censoring themselves to avoid conflict.** Maybe you still keep feeling that you can't raise questions without risking your spiritual standing in the community. If speaking up continues to get you shamed, sidelined or labeled as "divisive," you may need to prepare to move on.

- **Staying longer requires self-betrayal.** If you still feel that you must silence your conscience to stay, and you find yourself pretending in any way, you are at risk of getting emotionally bruised and burned out. Maybe you are being asked to protect power at the expense of people, and you know deep down that you would need to betray your own boundaries and values to do that.

- **You are paying an unhealthy cost for staying.** Maybe you have started feeling constant anxiety or spiritual exhaustion. Maybe you are noticing the impacts of this battle on your mental and physical health. Maybe the closest people around you are suffering as well.

- **You know that by staying, you enable harm.** Deep

down, you know that your loyalty to the system keeps the harm going. You know that if enough people walked away, the abuse of power would crumble, and more people would stay safe. You know that staying in a controlling and, therefore, abusive system sends a message outside that everything's fine within it, even though you know this is not true. The bigger this tension is inside of you, the clearer the message that it may be time to leave.

Leaving a faith community is never an easy choice. It can carry a lot of uncertainty and the ache of what's been lost, even when it is the only way towards healing. You may need to practice choosing the truth over denial and health over harm. Choosing to exit usually starts with sorrow, but can, over time, transform into a rediscovery of faith that restores.

It is very natural not to know if you are just overreacting or if what you are seeing around you is really that bad. I would encourage you to reach out to people outside of your community. Reach out to professionals like therapists, spiritual directors or coaches, and speak with former members about what you are sensing. If multiple voices confirm that *it's not you, it's the system,* believe them.

How Can We Support Someone in Leaving?

"All I needed was to talk about my experience
and for someone to listen."

I want to speak directly to *you* who are in the process of leaving a high-control group. Maybe you have tried to change things, or you have seen others who did and got their wings burned. Maybe you've already seen some cosmetic changes only and know there will be no genuine change. You know deep down that you won't be able to stay in a community that has made you smaller than you really are.

As you now know, the process of leaving a high-control group often begins with questions or small doubts. You may have often felt guilty about this and are now afraid to start thinking critically about some of the practices you have been witnessing. I want you to know that confusion is *a healthy, human response to control,* and you have permission to start trusting your own mind and discernment again. As Hebrews 5:14 says, "But solid food is for the mature, who by constant use have trained themselves to distinguish good from evil," you can start practicing distinguishing healthy practices from unhealthy ones. Your confusion is a sign that your mind is already taking its first steps towards breaking free from unquestioned obedience.

You may have been feeling layers of fear recently. I would like for you to know that the fear of isolation, fear of having no purpose or calling outside the group, or the fear of punishment and divine judgment are *tactics of control,* not an entire reality. You are very much loved by God, and he has promised you a lot. None of these promises are conditional on your staying in an abusive group. Keep in mind that, "I give them eternal life, and they shall never perish; no one will snatch them out of my hand. My Father, who has given them to me, is greater than all; no one can snatch them out of my Father's hand" (John 10:28-29).

What do you believe deep down? What feels true to you apart from the group's voice? Do you remember a time when everything felt clear and easy—what was different about that time to now? You have an inner compass, created and beautifully crafted by God, to help you discern between healthy and unhealthy discipleship. If you feel *disconnected from your discernment,* you may have been told to not trust your heart but to trust those who tell you what you should believe. Can you recognize this ever happening to you? Isaiah 30:21 reminds us that, "Whether you turn to the right or to the left, your ears will hear a voice behind you, saying, 'This is the way; walk in it.'" You can practice trusting this leading over the inherited expectations of your controlling community.

I know leaving can feel like betrayal. You may need to practice *reframing loyalty*. You asking questions means you are seeking the truth, and this is what integrity looks like. You have permission to stay loyal to what God is showing you, and how he is helping you study Scripture in context. You can grow in trusting your faith like Peter and the other apostles in Acts 5:29 did when he said, "We must obey God rather than human beings!"

I have met many people who have left high-control communities and are now thriving outside of them. Many of them walked through the valley of trauma healing first but came to the other side as whole, authentic believers now passionate about resisting these dynamics. Maybe you can connect with some of these people and hear their stories. I believe it's important for you to know that *you are not alone.* "Never will I leave you; never will I forsake you.' So we say with confidence, 'The Lord is my helper; I will not be afraid. What can mere mortals do to me?'" (Hebrews 13:5-6).

I do want to encourage you to find at least one safe person outside of your group to talk to. I would encourage you to study credible resources and learn more about control and religious trauma. You have permission to grow in wisdom in this season. "Do not forsake wisdom, and she will protect you; love her, and she will watch over you. The beginning of wisdom is this: Get wisdom. Though it cost all you have, get understanding" (Proverbs 4:6-7).

You have a choice in all of this. I know all this can feel quite overwhelming at first, but every small choice can be yours from now on. You can choose what to read, what to study, who to talk to, and how to spend your free time. You can choose to pray as someone who is not afraid anymore but totally and completely honest and transparent with God. Ask him to help you find the truth over indoctrination. "Show me your ways, LORD, teach me your paths. Guide me in your truth and teach me, for you are God my Savior, and my hope is in you all day long" (Psalm 25:4-5).

After you've chosen to leave, you will most likely *experience grief.* I understand there is a lot at stake here, and the loss is absolutely real and valid. Every meaningful change also brings considerable loss. Amid your grief, you can also allow yourself to imagine who you could become, what kinds of relationships you could have, and what kind of freedom you could experience moving forward. There is so much *hope* in this process as well, even if it's still hiding from you in some ways. Remember that Isaiah 41:10 says that "So do not fear, for I am with you; do not be dismayed, for I am your God. I will strengthen you and help you; I will uphold you with my righteous right hand."

Moving forward, after you've given yourself some time to heal, you may want to start listening to others hurt by control more intently, without judgment and with compassion and curiosity. Jesus often caused discomfort to those in power when he exposed what burdening practices and hypocrisy looked like. I have come to believe that in our pursuit to be more like him, we can no longer leave this part out. This invitation is for you as well.

Life After Leaving

"It's been so difficult
and it feels like it's taking forever to heal."

Stepping away from a controlling faith community can often come with a new, disorienting chapter. The world outside can feel unfamiliar, and the freedom you wanted still hides underneath incredible pain. What follows is the aftermath of loss, but also the opportunity to explore what a faith rooted in safety can look like.

Leaving can bring up a mixture of relief and upheaval, and it's important you know that all your responses are valid and a sign of you being a human being with a story. Many people experience a range of emotional, social, and practical shifts during this time. While the journey is different for everyone, there are some common experiences that can help you prepare and understand what to expect.

- **Emotional Whiplash.** You may find yourself swinging between exhilaration (I'm free!) and despair (What have I done?) after your exit. You can expect to feel confused, sad, scared, and lonely at first. This is what most must move through at first, but it is not the end stop.

- **Identity Rebuilding.** As we have discussed, much of people's identities are usually tied to these groups—they know how to define themselves through their communities, but not without them. After leaving, you will probably face a "Who am I?" crisis. It can feel quite daunting, but as you already know, there are ways to build back a whole identity that rests on the foundation of Scripture and healthy faith.

- **Grief and Loss.** Even though you may now see your former group of faith as harmful, you also know that's not the whole truth. You know there's always great loss as well. Leaving may have meant losing community, certainty, maybe even family ties, and sometimes a whole worldview. This part of the recovery process allows time for mourning.

- **Vulnerability to Replacement Groups.** Because of the loss and the hollow emptiness leaving often brings, you may be vulnerable to join another high-control environment or relationship, or you may regret leaving so much that you will want to go back. This can happen before healing is more on its way, and while living without the outside structures still feels too terrifying. Recovering, at this stage, means building back such sturdy internal structures that relying on outside ones doesn't feel as important anymore.

- **Residual Fear.** High-control cultures may have taught automatic fear responses to you, which have created perfectionism and people-pleasing behaviors as your survival mechanisms. Unlearning this takes time because fear can linger in the nervous system long after the threat is gone. This is a physiological issue, not a faith or character issue. These fears may still create nightmares, panic attacks, or anxiety about being outside of the will of God long after you have exited your faith community. Unlearning this will mean learning how to regulate your nervous system, and it would be a good idea to seek professional support for this.

- **Practical Rebuilding.** You may face some real challenges with the basics: finding housing, figuring out finances, getting educated and employed, and navigating systems and relationships you weren't allowed to engage with before. This can feel isolating and lonely at first and will call for great resilience. Groups of faith that recognize the need to support people like yourself going through this phase can be of great help. This would mean that leaders in healthy faith environments see this as an important issue and volunteer to support the exiles coming out of high-control faith cultures.

- **Permission to Heal at Your Own Pace.** High-control groups often view suffering as a character flaw or a faith issue and demand instant healing. The truth is that there is no timeline for recovery. Some of you may need distance and quiet, some may need to share their story many times for whoever might listen. Some of you will start to feel better in a short amount of time while others may need months or years to feel like themselves again. Both ways are just as valid.

- **Finding Freedom and Joy Again.** Freedom can look like connecting with the things that come naturally and without force again. It can be about exploration and finding purpose where your natural desires meet someone else's need in the world. There's real joy in doing what you are naturally good at and internally motivated in, while seeing how you can touch those who benefit from your gifts and talents.

Healing from Shame

"I'm starting to let people see me.
First, I had to learn to see myself."

As safety keeps growing and you start sharing your story, a new layer of healing often begins: the slow work of facing shame. As we've discussed, control-based systems thrive on shame because it keeps people quiet, small, and compliant.

Trauma shame is the deep sense of worthlessness or self-blame that often follows traumatic experiences. It moves in when we internalize the trauma and start to believe the event or series of events was our fault or that they mean something bad about who we are.

Using some of the tools by trauma expert Tim Fletcher, we will look at strategies for overcoming trauma shame. You can try some or all of them and see what works best for you.

As he notes, "Healing isn't about erasing shame. It's about developing a new relationship with it—where shame visits, but doesn't move in."[58]

1. Why "Just Love Yourself" Doesn't Work

Many of you may have been told, in a well-meaning manner, to just let go of the pain of the past. This doesn't often land well with individuals affected by trauma. This instead creates more shame.

The reason is not because people are flawed or have little faith. The reason is that shame always hides underneath trauma, and this is a sign of them needing some healing. And healing is always available.

Whenever individuals affected by shame try to force themselves to believe or feel loved, the Inner Critic usually jumps back on, saying, "You haven't done enough to deserve it. You need to do more and do it better."

When these old messages come back, the Child part doesn't need forced positivity, but to feel safe. And safety starts with radical acceptance, not performance.

2. Practice Acceptance (Where Child and Adult Meet)

Shame is the signal the Child part has gotten hurt and wounded, and the Inner Critic is now reinforcing the injury. It's not helpful to fight this shame by silencing either one. There's healing in letting the Adult self and a more nurturing voice take the wheel, practicing acceptance instead of suppression:

---

[58] Fletcher, Tim. "Will I Ever Heal from My Shame?' The Life-Changing Truth About Overcoming Toxic Shame,'" timfletcher.ca.

"I accept all my thoughts and feelings." (Even if my Inner Critic scoffs at them.)

"I accept my trauma and sensitivity." (Even if the world around me has punished me for both.)

"I accept my past." (Even if my Wounded Child still feels stuck there.)

"I accept all my doubts and questions." (Even if the environment around me tells me otherwise.)

You can move through acceptance like this:

• Name the Shame Story:

"I'm telling myself my thoughts, feelings, and behaviors mean I'm evil or too sinful."

• Notice the two ego states dialoguing:

"That's my Inner Critic talking."
"My Child ego state feels scared."

• Ask the Adult Questions:

"What would I say to a friend who felt this way?"
"Is there anything else that could be true here?"
"What does the Bible teach?"
"Does God love me as I am, or only when I perform perfectly?"
"Where did I learn this from, and do I still want this here?"

• Practice Self-Compassion:

"The Child in me needs me to defend him/her from this criticism."

And whenever shame and the Inner Critic come back saying, "You're too much," try this response from your healthy Adult: "Maybe at times, I am. But that's a sign of me being a human being with a story."

3. Practice Being Seen

Shame thrives in the shadows and silence. It wants to isolate, exclude, and move individuals away from connection. But once you learn to recognize its voice, you can stop letting it steer.

- Text a safe person: "I'm working on shame. Can I share something with you?"
- Call someone you trust and, with their permission, share about your struggles and how you are working through them.
- Meet up with a trusted friend and be open about what's going on with you.
- Write a note from your Adult self to your Inner Child.
- Next time shame flares, say: "This is my painful past learning. I don't do this to myself anymore."

And with all of this, you can talk to God about your shame. You can pray that he will show you everything that truly resides in your heart, so that you can work it through with him.

And you can take your time.

Chapter Sixteen

Psychologically Safe Faith Communities

*The Spirit you received does not make you slaves, so that you live in fear
again; rather, the Spirit you received brought about your adoption to sonship.*
– Romans 8:15

"For the first time ever,
I have been given freedom
to choose if I'm ready to participate."

Healthy faith communities stand in sharp contrast to controlling systems, even where control seems benign and subtle. Instead of demanding silence and conformity in countless ways, they welcome questions, differences, and our full stories as they are. When communities are built on the foundation of safety and trust, our relationships can be formed without fear of judgment or rejection. Faith is not a burden to carry anymore, but a source of life that flows without force.

Healthy faith communities are always quick to recognize who their practices and language protect: the ones in power or the ones who have been hurt. They will be active in moving away from keeping the harm going.

The Bible talks about the importance of gathering together, and for these gatherings to be lifegiving, we'll need to discuss how we relate to each other. We've already looked at how the Child can be internally quieted, and how we also quiet that part of us in relationships with other people. Both our internalized Parent and Child parts hold learned patterns of thinking, feeling, and behaving that didn't start with us.

Here, we will turn to what it can look like when the whole community commits to treating each other fairly, and build Adult leadership that can call forth the Adult state in others. This will help create a culture where control and abuse can't thrive. In this chapter, we'll explore some of the key principles that shape such communities and how they can bring more healing than harm.

Focus on Scripture

"It's taken so long
but I'm finally healing."

Healthy faith communities center their teaching on the contextual understanding of Scripture. They encourage members to engage with the Bible as a living word of God and recognize that it was written across different times, places, and genres, and that understanding these elements is essential for grasping the intended meaning. Their conviction is to teach Scripture for people to grow in their personal faith, instead of strengthening their own authority as leaders.

They want to teach Scripture as honestly as they possibly can. Teachers place biblical passages within their original audience, language, and cultural norms before applying them today. They avoid cherry-picking verses to enforce behavioral rules or emotional control. They also encourage people to explore different scholarly perspectives and approaches, and they don't shy away from the more challenging topics or the ones we often must wrestle with. Healthy teachers don't view themselves as unmistakable messengers of God's Word.

Healthy teachers also encourage everyone's personal engagement with Scripture and prayer. They create space for questions, doubts, and discussion without fear of judgment. They provide Bible study tools for individuals to study on their own and for their own benefit. They value the process of seeking God, not just having the "right" answers. Members are not expected to always land on similar interpretations of Scripture that always need to support the group's own doctrine, but instead are encouraged to grow in their personal, biblical discernment.

Healthy teachers also place relationships over rules and people over norms. They point toward love, justice, mercy, and humility before their own authority or members' unquestioned submission. They focus on teaching how faith can transform our hearts, but not on external conformity.

They also, of course, avoid misusing their power by using Scripture to silence, bypass, shame or force obedience. They make a clear distinction between biblical principles and human traditions.

For them, spiritual maturity and humility are more important than image, and growth is celebrated over perfectionism. Spiritual maturity is recognized as a lifelong journey marked by discerning God's voice, applying Scripture wisely, and loving others well.

Structures and Processes to Check

> "I've found a place where I don't have to
> constantly give to be seen as important."

Healthy faith communities focus on building psychological safety. Psychological safety is a sense within a group where it is okay to emotionally struggle, make mistakes, and not have all the answers, without needing to please or appease the people around them. It is one of the most critical aspects of any healthy culture or relationship, and is often diminished in controlling environments. In psychologically safe faith communities, people can be free to share things that bother them, scare them, or challenge them, without any fear of negative consequences.[59]

Our faith communities don't need to be perfect, but aiming for health should be a priority in our world today. Psychologically safe faith communities are trauma-informed, transparent, and honest, and intentionally move away from control toward freedom. They are rooted in truth: "Rather, we have renounced secret and shameful ways; we do not use deception, nor do we distort the word of God. On the contrary, by setting forth the truth plainly we commend ourselves to everyone's conscience in the sight of God" (2 Corinthians 4:2).

If you are at a spot where bringing change feels right to you, or you are trying to find a healthier church after exiting an abusive one, here are some structures and processes to keep an eye on. First, you would need to see willingness and humility to admit wrongdoings, and repentance from old ways. Next, you would need to see a willingness to engage in learning. Anything can be built anew when the heart takes this position.

A healthy and psychologically safe faith community structure is clear and transparent. People in the structure would know their role very well and are not expected to do more than handle their own responsibilities. They would be well-trained. You can discuss these points with the leadership team and assess their willingness and openness to change where change is needed. These are some of the more foundational pieces of any healthy structure, which you are free to examine:

1. Leadership Accountability

• In a healthy system, leaders are accountable to an independent body and not only to themselves or a small inner circle. You are free to ask directly who the leaders are accountable to. Is there an

---

[59] "What Is Psychological Safety?" *Psych Safety*, psychsafety.com.

elder board? Outside oversight? You can look for organizational charts or ask to see governance documents. Transparency in this area is a sign of health. Leaders who are committed to change are committed to setting external supervision to keep all levels of leadership accountable to someone.

• In a healthy system, there is transparency about finances, decision-making, and governance. You can request access to financial statements or ask how decisions are made. Are budgets available to members? Who makes the final calls?

2. Handling of Abuse

• Healthy structures hold clear processes for handling misconduct, and they have people responsible and trained to address such reports. There is an understanding and training of what the duty of care means. You are free to ask if allegations of abuse have been taken seriously, reported to appropriate authorities, and managed transparently. Healthy structures would include clear guidelines on how these situations are handled and the process is followed in a consistent manner each time. The top leaders are not exempt from honest evaluation and accountability.

• People in healthy structures understand the need to support those leaving high-control churches. Look for the openness to add the presence of support groups, licensed counselors, and trauma-informed staff. You will need to know who people can turn to in times of crisis. The wounded need tangible support structures, not just words. With any process, check who it protects: the victim or the one in power. Keep also in mind that these support mechanisms can't be used as band aids, where the issues of control remain, even though some sort of support is available. The root issue of control needs to be dealt with first.

3. Training of Staff

• You can check for the openness to bring outside trainers and professionals to train the whole staff on healthy governance, accountability and good mental health practices. This training could include equipping leaders and staff alike to recognize the differences between influence and manipulation, authority and authoritarianism, and guidance and coercion. The whole staff would need tools for fostering open dialogue, encouraging questions, and respecting individual autonomy, while still holding shared vision and values. Leadership committed to change would welcome such training and participate in it with the whole staff.

4. Language & Beliefs

• A faith community that's committed to change will take inventory of its collective beliefs and language together. They will be open to checking their teachings for loaded language and imposed expectations that may have been inherited instead of chosen. They would check if they had engaged in the misuse of Scripture.

• Some questions to talk through: Have fear-based messages been used to enforce compliance? Have guilt and shame been framed as spiritual virtues rather than warning signs of manipulation? Have people felt free to make their own choices without any high-control framing?

• Have those leaving the group been treated with kindness and respect, or as traitors and threats? Are friendships conditional on group membership? Lasting friendships that don't depend on conformity are a good sign of genuine connection. If people seem to feel they "don't have time" for building relationships outside of their group, it can reveal some levels of isolation, and all abusive systems isolate their members, whether knowingly or unknowingly.

• Does the group claim authority over non-religious aspects of people's lives, such as careers, education, relationships, living arrangements or personal choices? A community committed to change would be committed to respecting everyone's autonomy and boundaries.

When assessing the health of any faith community, you are also invited to look at both the stated beliefs and the practical culture: how the stated values are lived out. Systems often reveal their health in how their values are applied, how dissent is handled, and how leadership relates to members.

Real change doesn't mean surface-level tweaks but a deeper-level root search. A tree that develops both good and bad fruit is in desperate need of pruning. After your conversations with the leaders of your faith community, you will be able to tell if they are willing to transform their practices into something healthier.

People are always more important than any belief system. When our interpretation of the Bible drives us to pressure or control other people, it reveals that something has gone wrong in the way we're reading it. Scripture's purpose is to shape our own character, not to give us authority over someone else's freedom.

Trauma-Informed Communities

"After years of performing,
I have finally started making friends who really know me."

If you have experienced high-control and high-demand Christianity, it's possible that you may later down the track realize that you have experienced betrayal trauma. Institutional betrayal occurs when an individual has trusted or depended on an institution that ultimately mistreats them. This trauma can arise due to actions that harmed them, or from failing to act when action was expected—like mandatory reporting, following the law, and believing individuals reporting wrongdoings.

It will take time to rebuild trust, and groups of faith can help the hurting in many different ways. The more we understand the link between wounding and controlling faith environments, the better we will be at offering space for healing.

Trauma-informed practice is an approach to care, leadership, and community that recognizes the widespread impact of trauma and responds in ways that promote healing rather than retraumatization. Being trauma-informed means we take this matter seriously and center our work in our faith communities around these five principles: **Safety, Trustworthiness, Choice, Collaboration and Empowerment.**[60]

Trauma-informed ministry is not a separate program or something only some participate in, but a way of seeing other people around us, and the way of relating and being together. This needs to matter to the leadership first, who are responsible for creating a culture of safety in their churches, and honoring others above themselves (Romans 12:10).

---

[60] "What Is Trauma-Informed Care?" *University at Buffalo*, socialwork.buffalo.edu.

These principles can be modified to fit any faith community:

1. Safety

When individuals consider joining a church, they need to know that they will be heard, that support will be available, and that they will be treated fairly. They should be informed about the levels of accountability within the community—systems that are transparent and real. It's also essential that they understand the leadership structure of the congregation, including clear communication about how decisions are made, how conflict is handled, and how concerns can be raised without fear of retaliation or dismissal.

This is especially important for trauma survivors, who need to feel that systems are consistent and that leadership is approachable, not hierarchical in ways that create fear or silence. A culture of honest dialogue is one of the keys to building trust.

In practice, this kind of culture looks like clearly defined boundaries around pastoral relationships, respectful language, and teachings that avoid high-control framing. It includes creating space for people to step back, rest, or say "no" without fear of judgment or spiritual pressure.

Healthy communities are emotionally safe. In these spaces, feelings are not equated with faith in God. People are not gossiped about or excluded for being honest or emotionally vulnerable. Boundaries are honored, and grace is not only preached but practiced.

2. Trustworthiness

Therefore each of you must put off falsehood
and speak truthfully to your neighbor,
for we are all members of one body.
– Ephesians 4:25

When someone is trustworthy, they can be relied on as honest and truthful. They consistently are who they say they are and deliver on the promises they have made. Similarly, trustworthy faith communities speak the truth about Scripture and about their goals for people inside and outside their walls.

Healthy communities are marked by open and transparent communication. Building trustworthiness is a promise to avoid secrecy and high-control framing in communication. Leaders and members alike behave in ways that match their words, avoiding double standards or hidden agendas.

Instead of loaded language, communication is honest and accurate. People can also count on commitments being kept, whether that's confidentiality, promises, or pastoral care. Practices are aligned with the core values of the group.

Trustworthiness also means respecting confidentiality in conversations and a promise to keep people's stories private when asked. A culture like this never makes individuals repent in front of others or make decisions for them without their consent.

Also, when people understand what their faith community stands for and what is asked of them, they can make informed choices about their participation. Consent only exists when goals, expectations, and practices are clearly named from the beginning.

3. Choice

High-control framing often leaves people feeling powerless, because it opens the door to a space where real choices don't exist. Meaningful options in any faith community allow everyone to practice autonomy, make personal decisions without fear and move at their own pace. This can look like being invited to be the one to decide on the level of involvement that feels safe and sustainable to them and offering multiple ways to participate in church activities.

There's flexibility on ministry involvement, and people can choose how to engage in church service. Everyone has a choice in how much time and money they give; they can step back without threats of losing relationship, and they are encouraged to make personal decisions with the wisdom they have in themselves.

In healthy faith communities, faith is not measured by how closely someone mirror's others' beliefs or practices. Each person is free to discern what resonates with their values and conscience, and to engage at their own pace.

Reclaiming agency in faith allows people to trust their own convictions and to say no to practices that hurt or control others.

4. Collaboration

Now you are the body of Christ,
and each one of you is a part of it.
— 1 Corinthians 12:27

Collaboration creates shared ownership of ministry and reduces the risk of hierarchical control. This could look like ministry decisions being made in conversation with all staff, instead of coming from the top down. Leaders tend to work in teams and make decisions together. In this way, leaders would model humility and mutual respect, and show a willingness to learn from members, not just teach others.

Genuine collaboration would not place any one person spiritually above others. Collaboration acknowledges each individual's unique gifts as strengths and is willing to utilize them in ways that work best for each of them. Everyone's perspectives and abilities are valued in decision-making and day-to-day life.

5. Empowerment

By wisdom a house is built,
and through understanding it is established.
— Proverbs 24:3

Empowerment restores agency and reinforces individuality. It untangles the framing where critical thinking is seen as a sin and autonomy as rebellion. It breaks people free from enmeshed relationships and builds healthy boundaries again.

Leaders and members alike can practice asking others, "What would be most helpful for you now?" instead of imposing solutions they believe are best for the person. They can keep affirming people that asking questions and challenging some of the ideas of the faith community is welcomed and a sign of health.

Teachings can include an emphasis on everyone's God-given potential, where differences are seen as strengths. There will be more opportunities than there is gatekeeping; members are encouraged to lead initiatives and serve in ways that reflect their personal values.

In trauma-informed, safe communities, we can expect to see both growth and healing. In such spaces, our lived experiences are acknowledged, and we can keep exploring a faith that restores. We can express our emotions without fear and learn to trust again. Gradually, we are able to release the burdens of past harm and become fully seen and known.

Chapter Seventeen

Moving From Control to Freedom

You will seek me and find me when you seek me with all your heart.
I will be found by you, declares the Lord,
and will bring you back from captivity.
– Jeremiah 29:13-14

"I feel closer to God now than before I left."

We've come quite a long way, from recognizing control to naming the wounds to healing and building healthy faith communities together. At the beginning of this book, we looked at how the Pharisees felt about faith and how Jesus consistently responded to them. This is where we started:

1. It feels more important to be right about questions of theology than to remain in relationship with others. It feels appropriate to uphold black-and-white rules to test others, trying to catch them out, expecting them to be wrong in their beliefs, all while being "above" them. Control makes it difficult to recognize the unconventional moves of the Spirit while making it easy to spot "wrong" behavior (Matthew 23:23-24).

2. It is a culture of loaded language, where many spiritually-correct-sounding concepts are discussed with the help of Scripture, but where people's hearts may remain far from God (Matthew 7:21-23).

3. It feels right, appropriate, and even holy to observe whether other people are doing the right thing according to the rules and to report any shortcomings to their leaders (Matthew 12:2).

4. It feels important to do everything the way things have always been done, to follow the traditions and rules of the faith community, and to consider anything different as sinful or wrong (Matthew 15:7-9).

5. It creates a perspective that judges everything different from them and everyone who, in their eyes, sins. Those who judge others believe they are doing the right thing by adhering to the rules and calling others out (Matthew 7:1-5).

6. With all this in place, it creates a culture where people are taught to care more about how they present themselves to others and how they appear on the outside, rather than being open and honest about what is happening beneath the surface, deep in their hearts (Matthew 23:25-26).

These are some of the things we can see in the culture the Pharisees created:

- Parent-led leading style with black-and-white thinking
- Use of loaded language and misuse of Scripture
- Surveillance culture and behavioral policing
- Immovable, stagnant beliefs
- Strong Inner Critic rules that overflowed to others and built entire systems
- Strong emphasis on performance, effort, image, and popularity

The Pharisees burdened other believers probably because they were burdened themselves.

Spiritual burdens traumatize people.

Control is a burden.

Control traumatizes people.

With All our Heart, Soul, and Mind

When Jesus was asked to name the greatest commandment, he said:

*Love the Lord your God with all your heart and with all your soul and with
all your mind. This is the first and greatest commandment.
And the second is like it: Love your neighbor as yourself. All the Law and
Prophets hang on these two commandments.*
– Matthew 22:37-40

This command is rooted in choice, not fear or coercion. We can't manufacture love for God, ourselves or others through pressure, and we can't maintain it through control, not even when we do all the "right" things and appear strong in our faith.

The invitation to honest love welcomes our whole selves into the relationship with God and others, not just our compliant selves. When we love God with all our hearts, we bring him everything that's in them: their joys, disappointments, sorrows, fears, questions, passions and pains. When we love him with all our minds, we start engaging with our intellect, reasoning, and curiosity again. We seek the truth over doctrine, and relationship over fear.

Walking with God with our whole heart, soul, and mind is an invitation into wholeness. Loving him with all of ourselves means bringing the parts of us that have been shut down, dismissed, shamed, or labeled as rebellious back into the relationship with him.

Without choice, love becomes unsafe. Without curiosity,

faith becomes pressured. Without emotional honesty, our relationship with God becomes more of a performance than a meeting place.

As we have discussed all throughout this book, high-control systems present devotion as a narrow path of prescribed "choices," where the measure of faith is to always do the "right" thing, whatever it may be. In such systems, freedom is replaced with moral obligation.

Jesus came to free us from captivity. Freedom in Christ is available to all of us, but we will need to make our own independent choice to seek it.

The invitation to a transformative relationship with him starts with your choice. Come as you are. Think freely. Feel deeply. Walk authentically with him.

Healed by Grace

Whoever believes in me, as Scripture has said,
rivers of living water will flow from within them.
— John 7:38

There is an invitation for you to start tearing down the rules and unbearable expectations that have been placed over you like a heavy blanket and finally break free from their pressure.

There is a whole life waiting for you outside of the tight boxes you have felt you have had to mold yourself into for the sake of the acceptance of those around you.

There is a possibility of hearing God's voice more clearly without the internalized rules that have held you captive.

There is transparency, maturity, and wholeness available to you.

There is also the freedom to make mistakes, stumble, and grow without fear of judgment.

There is peace in learning to listen to God's guidance in your own heart, even when it goes against the culture's expectations.

There is joy in discovering your unique gifts and allowing them to grow through your service to God.

There is rest available to you.

There is trust that even through hardships, God's love will keep leading you to repentance and a life of honest transformation and freedom, no matter where you are placed in the world.

You can leave control behind you and be who you are.
You can take time for your bruises to heal.
You can love the people around you in your everyday life, wherever you are, at any time.

As you keep moving towards freedom,
I pray the Lord may bless you, and keep you.
May the Lord make his face shine on you,
And be gracious to you.
May the Lord turn his face toward you,
And give you peace.
Amen.

Thank you

First, to my husband, Vesku – you are the most honest and transparent person I have ever known. Thank you for always being exactly who you say you are. You are my best friend, my support, and my greatest encourager.

To my teenagers, Max and Mila – you are both courageous thinkers, genuine to the core, and you love God and others so naturally. Words can't begin to express how proud I am of you both. Your friends are extremely lucky to know you.

To my parents – thank you for teaching me critical thinking skills from a young age, and for helping me get to this point in life. Your prayers of blessing have carried the four of us over many hurdles.

To our extended family back home – we miss you all so much.

To my friends all over the world who have always been there for me – you're all amazing. I feel honored to call you my friends.

To our pastor at The Rocks, Daniel Indradjaja – thank you for being a steady support, for reading my manuscript, for praying with us through difficult seasons, and for always being rooted in truth.

To my editor, Kelly Freestone – thank you for your patience throughout the creative process and for your guidance when I needed it.

To Nick Gwynn, Director at Breathe Counselling – you've been a great leader these past four years. Thank you for trusting me.

To Samuel Ingram, Graphic Designer at Breathe Counselling – thank you for your creativity and skill in creating this beautiful book cover.

To my supervisors, Linda Gregory and Jan Coleman – I've grown immensely through the opportunity to work with both of you.

To all the people and situations in my life, past and present – each has led me here. Some I wish had never happened, and yet, I'm glad they did. My heart has at least tripled in size because of it all.

Thank you, Jesus. I love you.